MACHINE LEARNING USING PYTHON:

Discover the world of Machine Learning using Python algorithm analysis, ide and libraries. Projects focused on beginners.

ERIC CHAMBERLIN

ERIC CHAMBERLIN

© Copyright 2020 - All rights reserved.

The content contained within this book may not be reproduced, duplicated or transmitted without direct written permission from the author or the publisher.

Under no circumstances will any blame or legal responsibility be held against the publisher, or author, for any damages, reparation, or monetary loss due to the information contained within this book. Either directly or indirectly.

Legal Notice

This book is copyright protected. This book is only for personal use. You cannot amend, distribute, sell, use, quote or paraphrase any part, or the content within this book, without the consent of the author or publisher.

Disclaimer Notice

Please note the information contained within this document is for educational and entertainment purposes only. All effort has been executed to present accurate, up to date, and reliable, complete information. No warranties of any kind are declared or implied. Readers acknowledge that the author is not engaging in the rendering of legal, financial, medical or professional advice. The content within this book has been derived from various sources. Please consult a licensed professional before attempting any techniques outlined in this book.

By reading this document, the reader agrees that under no circumstances is the author responsible for any losses, direct or indirect, which are incurred as a result of the use of information contained within this document, including, but not limited to, — errors, omissions, or inaccuracies.

ERIC CHAMBERLIN

Table of Contents

- INTRODUCTION 8
- **CHAPTER 1: MACHINE LEARNING HISTORY** 10
- **CHAPTER 2: WHAT IS MACHINE LEARNING?** 14
  - What is Machine Learning? 14
  - When Should We Use Machine Learning? 15
  - Steps in Building a Machine Learning System 18
- **CHAPTER 3: CATEGORIES OF MACHINE LEARNING** 22
  - Supervised Machine Learning 22
  - Unsupervised Machine Learning 24
  - Reinforcement Learning 27
- **CHAPTER 4: SECTORS AND INDUSTRIES THAT USE M.L** 32
  - Healthcare 33
  - Drug Manufacturing and Discovery 33
  - Personalized Medication or Treatment 34
  - Finance 34
  - Retail 35
  - Statistical Arbitrage 36
  - Prediction 36
- **CHAPTER 5: INTRODUCTION TO PROGRAMMING LANGUAGES** 38
  - Knowing Some of the Features of This Library 40
- **CHAPTER 6: WHY PYTHON** 44
  - Simple and Easy to Learn 44
  - High-level Language 44
  - Fast and Efficient to Use 44
  - Open Source 45
  - Interpreted 45
  - Object Oriented 46
  - Portable 46
  - Batteries Included 46
  - Numpy, Panda and Scikit-learn 47
  - Improved Productivity 47
  - Easy Learnability 48
  - Easy Readability 48
  - Wide Support of Major Platforms 48
  - Software Quality 48

CHAPTER 7: INSTALLING SCIKIT-LEARN 50
WHAT IS SCIKIT-LEARN? 50
UNDERSTANDING MORE ABOUT TENSOR FLOW 51
GETTING STARTED WITH SCIKIT-LEARN 53

CHAPTER 8: IDE (SPYDER, JUPITER) 62
PYTHON INTERPRETER, IDLE, AND THE SHELL 62

CHAPTER 9: INTRODUCTION TO THE MAIN PYTHON LIBRARIES 72
KERAS 72
THEANO 72
TENSORFLOW 73
SCIKIT-LEARN 73

CHAPTER 10: INTRODUCTION TO BIAS AND VARIANCE 76

CHAPTER 11: EVALUATING THE ERROR IN THE REGRESSION MODELS (RMSE, MAE, R2) 78
REGRESSION ANALYSIS 79
TESTING WITH R^2 CORRELATION: 83

CHAPTER 12: SUPERVISED LEARNING 86
SUPERVISED LEARNING ALGORITHMS 87

CHAPTER 13: LINEAR REGRESSION 92
CHOOSING THE BEST REGRESSION MODEL 94
STATISTICAL METHODS USED TO FIND THE BEST REGRESSION MODEL 94
FINDING THE CORRECT REGRESSION MODEL 96

CHAPTER 14: RANDOM FORESTS -THEORY 100
HOW TO INTERPRET RANDOM FORESTS 102

CHAPTER 15: EVALUATION METRICS AND CLASSIFICATION MODELS 106
MODEL EVALUATION 106

CHAPTER 16: UNSUPERVISED LEARNING 110
UNSUPERVISED LEARNING ALGORITHMS 110

CHAPTER 17: DEEP LEARNING 116
CLASSIFICATION 117
PATTERN RECOGNITION 119

CHAPTER 18: LOGISTIC REGRESSION-THEORY 122

CHAPTER 19: KNN -THEORY 126
CHAPTER 20: SUPPORT VECTOR MACHINES CLASSIFICATION 128
CHAPTER 21: REINFORCEMENT MACHINE LEARNING ALGORITHMS 132

- How Clustering Algorithms Work 132
- Types of Clustering Algorithms 133
- Application of Clustering Algorithms: 136
- When to use Clustering Algorithms? 137

CHAPTER 22: NAIVE BAYES -THEORY 138

- Naïve Bayes Estimation and Bayesian Networks 138

CHAPTER 23: DECISION TREES -THEORY 144

- Classification Using Decision Tree 144
- Decision Tree Construction 147
- Decision Tree Algorithm 148

CHAPTER 24: BENEFITS OF MACHINE LEARNING 150
CHAPTER 25: DEEP NEUTRAL NETWORK 152

- Neural networks 152
- Feedforward Neural Networks 156
- Single-layer perceptron 157
- Multi-layer Perceptron 157
- Recurrent Neural Networks 158
- Backpropagation 158

CHAPTER 26: BIG DATA ANALYTICS 162

- Volume 163
- Velocity 163
- Variety 164
- Value 164
- Veracity 164
- Current uses of Big Data. 165

CHAPTER 27: DATA MINING AND APPLICATIONS 170

- How Does Data Mining Work? 171
- Unbalanced Data Set 177

CONCLUSION 178

ERIC CHAMBERLIN

Introduction

Python Programming Language is basically interpreted in nature. As such, before one launch or run the code given, one needs to compile all the written code at once for onward interpretation through the 'print' command. Meanwhile, with Python, you as a programmer can help greatly with the growth of background for different software design. The process of abstracting details is a mechanism that serves as the core focal point for Python that even novice can understand.

Python will always be the choice of programmers because of its high rate in enhancing productivity. The steps in Python are edit, test and debug, respectively. Interestingly, a mistake in the code input of Python will never result in segmentation with a fault; this has made many programmers resort to the fact that it is one of the easiest languages for debugging. Instead of creating through the interpreter a segmentation with fault, python would rather develop a form of exception. If this exception is not still captured, it will be printed as a stacked race –just to keep everything safe.

You can confidently say that any change made to the structure of the machine, the data composition, or the data stored in the machine to improve the performance and accuracy of a machine is a sign of learning. When you try to better understand the concept of Machine Learning, you will realize that only some of these changes can be categorized as Machine Learning. For instance, let us look at a machine that is being used to forecast the weather in a specific region for a specific time frame.

So, without any further ado, let us begin.

CHAPTER 1:

Machine Learning History

The history of Machine Learning begins with the history of computing. And this history began before computers were even invented. The function of computers is actually math, in particular, Boolean logic. So, before anyone could create a computing machine, the theory about how such a machine could work had to be figured out by mathematicians. It was the growth of this theory from hundreds of years ago that made possible the revolution in computer software that we see today. In a way, the present and future of computing and Machine Intelligence belong to great minds from our past.

In 1957, Frank Rosenblatt, while working at the Cornell Aeronautical Laboratory, creates the perceptron. It is an algorithm that through supervised learning is able to "learn" to use binary classifiers to decide if an input (vector of numbers) belongs to a particular class. The perceptron caused something of a storm in the media, leading some to suggest the navy (the project was funded by the US Office of Naval Research) would soon have a machine that could, as the New York Times put it at the time, "walk, talk, see, write, reproduce itself, and be conscious of its existence." Unfortunately, the hype was all... hype. The perceptron hit a wall when researches working with it discovered it could only be trained to learn a small number of classes of patterns. This caused the field to stagnate for many years.

Eventually, this focus on a logical, knowledge-based approach to Artificial Intelligence caused a split between the disciplines. Machine Learning systems suffered from practical and theoretical problems in representation and acquiring large data sets to work with. Expert systems came to dominate by 1980, while statistical and probabilistic systems like Machine Learning fell out of favor. Early neural network research was also abandoned by Artificial Intelligence researchers and became its own field of study.

Machine Learning became its own discipline, mostly considered outside the purview of Artificial Intelligence, until the 1990s. Practically, all of the progress in Machine Learning from the 1960s through to the 1990s was theoretical, mostly statistics and probability theory. But while not much seemed to be accomplished, the theory and algorithms produced in these decades would prove to be the tools needed to re-energize the discipline. At this point, in the 1990s, the twin engines of vastly increased computer processing power and the availability of large datasets brought on a sort of renaissance for Machine Learning. Its goals shifted from the general notion of achieving Artificial Intelligence to a more focused goal of solving real-world problems, employing methods it would borrow from probability theory and statistics, ideas generated over the previous few decades. This shift and the subsequent successes it enjoyed, brought the field of Machine Learning back into the fold of Artificial Intelligence, where it resides today as a sub-discipline under the Artificial Intelligence umbrella.

However, Machine Learning was, continues to be, and might remain a form of Specific Artificial Intelligence (SAI). SAI are software algorithms that are able to learn a single or small range of items, which cannot be generalized to the world at large. The ultimate goal of Artificial Intelligence research is to develop a Generalized Artificial Intelligence (GAI), which will not only be able to learn about the world but to generalize that knowledge and use it to learn about new things it has never encountered before. To this date, GAI remains an elusive goal, one many believe will never be reached. However, this does not take away from the fact that Machine Learning algorithms, even if they are specific Artificial Intelligence (SAI), are changing the world and will have an enormous effect on the future.

CHAPTER 2:

What is Machine Learning?

What is Machine Learning?

Machine learning is a branch of Artificial Intelligence that involves the design and development of systems capable of showing an improvement in performance based on their previous experiences. This means that when reacting to the same situation, a machine should show an improvement from time to time. With Machine Learning, software systems are able to predict accurately without having to be programmed explicitly. The goal of Machine Learning is to build algorithms which can receive input data then use statistical analysis so as to predict the output value in an acceptable range.

Machine learning originated from pattern recognition and the theory that computers are able to learn without the need for programming them to perform any tasks. Researchers in the field of Artificial Intelligence wanted to determine whether computers are able to learn from data. Machine learning is an iterative approach, and this is why models are able to adapt as they are being exposed to new data. Models learn from their previous computations so as to give repeatable, reliable results and decisions.

When Should We Use Machine Learning?

When you have a problem that requires long lists of rules to find the solution.

Classification

In data science, more specifically in the fields of statistics and Machine Learning, classification is a type of problem where a particular observation, or data point, is placed into a category where it belongs, on the basis of similar characteristics, which in this case is based on the training set fed to the program, which contains instances or observations which the program can identify the membership of the said data points. One common example of a classification output in action would be an electronic mail spam filter, which classifies our electronic mail into one of two categories: "spam" (unwanted e – mail), and non – spam (legitimate e – mail messages). A more advanced type of classification in Machine Learning is how some new programs are trying to provide diagnostic services, and they provide diagnoses based on recorded symptoms of the patient as well as certain factors such as age, sex, and race, which allows the program to better predict the likely diagnosis.

Classification is mainly a type of pattern recognition, and is usually created through a supervised learning method, where the algorithm is taught using a set of data points where properly identified and categorized learning is already available. Classifiers are algorithms that implements the classification method, but the term "classifier" is also used in order to refer to a mathematical function that directs and categorizes input data into a certain category, but for the purposes of this guide, classifiers are classification method algorithms. Classifiers are usually created by splitting data points into certain variables, which may have various properties, such as categorical properties of blood types *"A -", "O +", "AB +"), ordinal (tall, regular, short), or even integer – valued (such as for spam filters which count for the number of occurrences of particular words). Some other classifiers are built using comparative observation, which have a function that compares distance or similarity between the two.

Clustering

Much like classification, clustering involves grouping together particular data points or observations based on a list of characteristics that would make them belong to the same category. However, clustering tends to be of a broader scope, and less clear – cut as compared to how classification decides to segment its categories. Clustering, or cluster analysis is mostly used by statisticians and data scientists, especially when it comes to solving problems of information retrieval, data compression, or density estimation functions. As was briefly explained earlier, the clustering function is usually created through an unsupervised Machine Learning algorithm, as compared to classification functions created through supervised learning. This is because clustering does not emphasize specificity as much and works more to gather similar objects together rather than individually define each object into a specific class.

Density Estimation

In what is basically a sub – type of clustering, the density estimation output method is an estimate built based on various observations, of an underlying probability density function, which is often unobservable. This function usually takes random samples from a population, and using the random sample, the unobservable density function that is to be estimated tends to be the density distribution of the larger population.

Dimensionality Reduction

Dimensionality reduction is a type of output that tries to reduce the complexity of objects and simplifies the input by mapping them into a lower-dimensional space, which eventually allows the user to simplify the objects and allow them to undergo feature selection or extraction, which is the process of identifying the most relevant attributes, or "features", in order to be better able to build a model. This is useful especially since there tends to be a problem in the increase of available dimensions and as such, sparser relevant data when objects are placed in high-dimensional space, so dimensionality reduction is often a necessary factor to making objects more accessible and useable.

Steps in Building a Machine Learning System

Regardless of the type of model that you are trying to build or the problem that you are trying to solve, you will follow the steps mentioned in this section while building a Machine Learning algorithm.

Define Objective

The first step, as it is with any other task that you perform, is to define the purpose or the objective you want to accomplish using your system. This is an important step since the data you will collect, the algorithm you use, and many other factors depend on this objective.

Collect Data

Once you have your objective in mind, you should collect the required data. It is a time-consuming process, but it is the next important step that you must achieve. You should collect the relevant data and ensure that it is the right data for the problem you are trying to solve.

Prepare Data

This is another important step, but engineers often overlook it. If you do overlook this step, you will be making a mistake. It is only when the input data is clean and relevant that you will obtain an accurate result or prediction.

Select Algorithm

Numerous algorithms can be used to solve a problem, including Structured Vector Machine (SVM), k-nearest, Naive-Bayes and Apriori, ***etc.*** You must choose the algorithm that best suits the objective.

Train Model

When your data set is ready, you should feed it into the system and help the machine learn using the chosen algorithm.

Test Model

When your model is trained, and you believe that it has provided the relevant results, you can test the accuracy of the model using a test data set.

Predict

The model will perform numerous iterations with the training data set and the test data set. You can look at the predictions and provide feedback to the model to help it improve the predictions that it makes.

Deploy

Once you have tested the model and you are happy with how it works, you can sterilize that model and integrate it into any application that you want to use. This means that the model that you have developed can now be deployed.

The steps followed will vary depending on the type of application and algorithm that you are using. You can choose to use a supervised or unsupervised Machine Learning algorithm. The steps mentioned in this section are often the steps followed by most engineers when they are developing a Machine Learning algorithm. There are numerous tools and functions that you can use to build a Machine Learning model. This book will help you with understanding more about how you can design a Machine Learning model using Python.

CHAPTER 3:

Categories of Machine Learning

Supervised Machine Learning

Supervised Machine Learning algorithms use the training data set to help a machine learn. This training data set will contain different input and output variable sets, and these sets are known as supervisory signals. An engineer uses this type of learning if he or she wants to generate or predict the output using a pre-existing function. If the data set is discrete, the function is called a classifier, and if the data set is continuous, the function is called a regressor. Every supervised Machine Learning algorithm has a generalized method that the machine can use to obtain or predict the desired output. The supervised Machine Learning algorithm works in the following manner:

- Once the engineer has identified the problem, he or she should determine the different examples, which can be used to help the machine learn. The engineer should also be extremely careful about the training data set that is being used since the machine will only learn from that data set.

- The engineer should identify the correct data set that can be used to solve the problem and scrub the data so it can be used to train the machine. The data set that the engineer uses should include all possible functions and outputs that the machine should look at. The engineer should also ensure that every input variable is mapped to the corresponding output variable.

- In this step, the engineer should choose the input data set that they should provide to the machine. It is important to provide the right data set to the machine since this will affect the performance of the model. The input variables used are provided in the form of a vector, and this vector possesses all the information about the characteristics and properties of the input variable. The engineer must then teach the machine how it should choose the necessary variables to obtain the desired output. If the machine cannot identify the right variables to use, it will provide incorrect outputs.

- It is only the engineer who can decide what the structure of the function can be. This function is dependent on the data set being used. The engineer should feed this function to the machine to help it obtain the required output.

- The engineer should now complete the design of the model. To do this, the engineer should first run the algorithm on the data set. He or she can also enter different parameters to control the working of the algorithm. Experts recommend that an engineer should use cross-validation methods to estimate the output. With this technique, the data set is split into small subsets, which makes it easy to estimate the parameters.

- When the algorithm runs, and the machine generates a function, the engineer can identify a way to test the performance and the accuracy of the model. For this purpose, the engineer can use a testing data set and verify if the model performs well and predicts the right outcome.

Numerous supervised Machine Learning algorithms can be used to solve different problems, and each of these algorithms has its respective pros and cons. It is important that the engineer chooses the correct algorithm to solve a problem.

Unsupervised Machine Learning

Unsupervised Machine Learning algorithms are different from supervised Machine Learning algorithms in the sense that the former will help the machine learn how to predict the outcome using a data set without any labels. These algorithms cannot be applied to regression and classification problems since you do not let the machine know what the output should be. It is for this reason that it becomes difficult to train the machine in the usual manner. These algorithms are often used to uncover the underlying relationships and structure within the data set. You can derive the approximation of results for any data set using supervised Machine Learning algorithms. As mentioned earlier, an unsupervised Machine Learning algorithm helps to uncover the underlying relationship within the data set. It is hard to determine if the result obtained is accurate since you are unaware of what the outcome should be. It is for this reason that most engineers prefer using supervised Machine Learning algorithms for real-world problems. If the data set provided does not have sufficient data, you should use an unsupervised Machine Learning algorithm. For instance, you can use an unsupervised Machine Learning algorithm if you want to identify the right time to launch a new product into the market. If you want to learn more about your customer base, you should use a supervised Machine Learning algorithm.

There are many applications or uses of unsupervised Machine Learning algorithms:

- Since most data have numerous variables, the clustering algorithm helps to split the data into multiple data sets based on the similarity that exists between these variables. Cluster analysis does tend to overestimate the similarities that exist between different variables in the data set. It is for this reason that most engineers do not choose to perform cluster analysis on their data sets, especially if they are looking to create customer segments.

- You can also identify any irregularities within the data set using anomaly detection. This allows different companies to identify fraudulent transactions, identify faulty hardware or tools, or even identify outliers or errors due to human prediction.

- You can identify the different types of items that occur in the data set using association mining. Retailers often use this approach when they perform basket analysis since that allows them to identify the list of items that a specific customer or a group of customers purchase at a specific point in time. This will allow the retailer to work on various branding and marketing strategies.

- You can use different latent variable models if you want to reduce the number of features within the data set or if you want to break the data set into different components.

- You can implement a supervised Machine Learning algorithm based on the information that you obtain from an unsupervised Machine Learning algorithm. For example, an unsupervised Machine Learning algorithm can be used to identify the clusters within a data set. These clusters can be used as additional input while developing a supervised Machine Learning algorithm.

Reinforcement Learning

Reinforcement learning is another branch of Machine Learning, and in this type of learning, the machine works towards maximizing the reward it receives by performing the right action in any situation. Many engineers use this type of learning where they allow a machine to identify the right behavior or action that it should take in any situation. Reinforcement learning and supervised Machine Learning is very different. The latter gives the machine a training data set, which also provides the required output to the machine. The former does not give the machine any answers. The machine should decide what it must do to obtain the results. The machine will only learn from its own experiences since there is no training data provided.

In the example below, there is a reward and there is an agent. There are many obstacles placed between the machine or agent, and the reward. The machine or agent should identify the right path that it should take to reach the reward in the shortest time possible. The image below will provide some information about this problem:

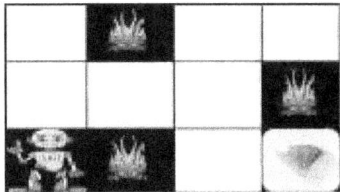

In the image above, there is a robot, which is the machine or agent, the fire that represents the obstacles and the diamond, which represents the reward. The robot should look for the different ways it can reach the diamond while avoiding fire. The aim should be to reach the diamond in the shortest time possible. The robot is rewarded for every correct step taken, and for every incorrect step it takes the reward is reduced. The total reward is calculated when the robot finally reaches the diamond.

Reinforcement Learning Process

- Input: The start from where the model begins to run is called the input.

- Output: Since there are many solutions to a problem, the model can choose or predict different outputs.

- Training: The model is trained based on the input data that is being taken to solve the problem. The engineer or the user can choose to reward or punish the model depending on the output that is returned to the user.

- Learning: The model will learn from every reward.

- Solution: Based on the reward that the model receives, it will decide the best solution that it should follow to solve the problem.

Types of Reinforcement

There are two types of reinforcement learning.

Positive

The model will always try to maximize the strength and frequency of a behavior that leads to a specific event. This means that this type of learning will always give the model a positive experience. The advantages of positive reinforcement learning are:

The model will learn to adapt to any changes or updates made to the data set.

Improves the performance and accuracy of the model.

The disadvantages of this type of learning are:

If the model is rewarded too many times, it will result in an overload in all the states.

Negative

Negative reinforcement learning helps the model strengthen the behavior that helps to prevent a negative outcome. The advantages of this type of learning are:

Improves the performance of the model by allowing it to defy a method.

It will increase the frequency of the behavior.

The disadvantages of this type of learning are:

This will allow the model just to provide enough to meet the minimum behavior.

ERIC CHAMBERLIN

CHAPTER 4:

Sectors and Industries that use M.L

Machine Learning helps to change how businesses work and operate in today's world. Through Machine Learning, large volumes of data can be extracted, which makes it easier for the user to draw some predictions from a data set.

There are numerous manual tasks that one cannot complete within a stipulated time frame if the task includes the analysis of large volumes of data. Machine Learning is the solution to such issues. In the modern world, we are overwrought with large volumes of data and information, and there is no way a human being can process that information. Therefore, there is a need to automate such processes, and Machine Learning helps with that.

When any analysis or discovery is automated fully, it will become easier to obtain the necessary information from that analysis. This will also help the engineer automate any future processes. The world of business analytics, data science, and big data requires Machine Learning and deep learning. Business intelligence and predictive learning are no longer restricted to just large businesses but are accessible to small companies and businesses too. This allows a small business to utilize the information that it has collected effectively. This section covers some of the applications of Machine Learning in the real world.

Healthcare

Doctors and practitioners can now predict how long a patient, suffering from terminal illnesses, will live with high accuracy. Medical systems are being designed to learn from training data. These machines also help a patient save money by avoiding unnecessary tests. Machine learning algorithms can now perform the task of a radiologist. It is believed that Machine Learning, when used to make medical decisions, can save up to $100 billion which could then be used to create novel tools for insurers, patients and doctors. It is true that machines and robots cannot replace doctors and nurses; nevertheless, the use of technology to save lives will transform the healthcare industry.

Drug Manufacturing and Discovery

It is an expensive and lengthy process to discover and manufacture a new drug since hundreds and thousands of compounds must be subjected to tests. There is a possibility that only one of the many drugs being tested can be used as a drug. Some Machine Learning algorithms can be used to improve the process.

Personalized Medication or Treatment

When you have an ache in your stomach or your head, you walk into your doctor's office and tell him your symptoms. Your doctor inputs those symptoms into the computer and narrows down on a probable cause. The system may also provide the doctor with the latest research on what he needs to know about the problem. He may ask you to take an MRI, and the computer will help the radiologist identify the problem if it is too hard for the human eye to identify. In the end, the computer will use your health records and your family medical history; compare it to the latest results and advise treatment for you. Machine learning helps to make treatment and medication more personal.

Personalized treatment will grow in the future, and Machine Learning will play a vital role in finding what genes or genetic markers are responsible for the diseases, and which ones will respond to the treatment.

Finance

Over 90% of the top financial institutions and organizations in the world use Machine Learning and advanced data analytics. Through Machine Learning, banks have developed the ability to offer personalized services to customers with better compliance and lower costs. They are also able to generate higher revenue.

Machine learning also helps in detecting fraud. For example, you are sitting at home and watching an episode of Game of Thrones when you get a call from your banker asking you if you have made a purchase of $Y in a store near your home. However, you did not make that purchase using your card, and the card is with you, so why did the bank flag this purchase alone? Machine Learning has something to do with this.

The finance and banking sectors use Machine Learning to combat fraud. It is best to use Machine Learning since it can scan through large volumes of transactional data and detect or identify any unusual behavior. A transaction made by a customer is often analyzed in real-time, and a score is given to that transaction to represent how fraudulent it may be. If the score is above a threshold, the machine will flag the transaction.

Retail

The Realities of Online Personalization Report stated that close to 45% of retailers are using Machine Learning to provide their customers with product recommendations that are based on the user's shopping history. Every customer looks for a personal shopping experience, and the recommendations always increase the conversion rates, thereby increasing the revenue for retailers.

Statistical Arbitrage

Statistical Arbitrage, a term often used in finance, refers to trading strategies that are used to identify the short-term securities that can be invested in. In these strategies, the user always tries to implement an algorithm on an array of securities that are based on the general economic variables and historical correlation of the data. The measurements are cast as estimation or classification problems. The basic assumption made is that the price will always move towards a historic average.

Machine learning methods are applied to obtain a strategy called the index arbitrage. Linear regression and support vector regression is used at different prices of a fund and on a stream of stocks, and then the Principal Component Analysis is used to reduce the dimensions in the dataset. The residuals are modeled to identify the trading signals as a mean-reverting process.

Prediction

Let us assume that a bank is trying to calculate the probability of a loan applicant defaulting on a repayment. To calculate this probability, the system will first have to identify, clean, and classify the data that is available in groups. This classification is performed based on certain criteria set out by the analysts. Once the classification of data is completed, the probability can be calculated. These calculations can be made across different sectors for a variety of purposes.

Prediction is one of the sought-after Machine Learning algorithms. If you were to look at a retailer, you can get reports on the sales that happened in the past. This type of reporting is called historical reporting. Now, you can predict the future sales of the company, which will help the business make the right decisions in the future.

CHAPTER 5:

Introduction to Programming Languages

There are a lot of things that you are going to enjoy when it comes to the Scikit-Learn environment and library. This is one of the best options that you can work with through Python and will make your Machine Learning projects so much more successful than before. If you are a programmer who is learning how to work with the process of Machine Learning, or you want to do more with your Python codes, then you need to make sure you have a good understanding of this library and how it works.

The Scikit-Learn library was developed in 2007. Later, the company started growing and made a lot of changes over time. Currently, it gets to enjoy more than 30 active contributors, and there are even some paid sponsorships from the INRIA, Google, and the Python Software Foundation to ensure that this library is going to be developed. And it is all done in a way that ensures that the user is not going to have to pay to use it! But this starts to bring up some questions about this library, and what it is all about. This library is going to ensure that the computer programmer has a lot of algorithms for both the unsupervised learning and the supervised learning that they want to do. And these algorithms are adjusted so that they can stay consistent with the Python environment. This means that you can use these algorithms and work on some Machine Learning projects all on Python.

This particular library is going to be licensed under what is known as a permissive simplified BSD license, and many of the Linux distributions can use it as well. It will be built using the SciPy library that will help make things even easier. The stack that is found inside of this, and which you will find helpful when you are working with Machine Learning includes:

- NumPy: This is a good one to use because it allows you to work on the n-dimensional array package

- SciPy: This one is going to be a fundamental library to use if you wish to do computations in the scientific field

- Matplotlib: This is a good library to use because it helps you do some plotting, whether in 2D or 3D.

- iPython: This is a good library to use because it is going to allow you a console that is more enhanced and interactive than others.

- Sympy: This is a library that works well if you want to do some things in symbolic mathematics.

- Pandas: This is the number one part that you need to use because it is going to include all of the analysis and the data structure needed to make Machine Learning successful.

The different extensions and modules that you can use with SciPy are known collectively as SciKits. This is why the module that provides us with the learning algorithms needed are going to be called the Scikit-Learn library.

The vision that is going to come in with this library will include a lot of support and robustness than you can find with some of the other topics that you explore. This is a good thing because both of these are going to require some higher levels to make sure that the production system works the way we expect and want. When going through this process, there has to be a deeper focus on the concerns, including ease of use, the collaboration, documentation, code quality, and performance, or it isn't going to work the way we want.

Knowing Some of the Features of This Library

At this point, we have talked a bit about this library, but we haven't gone into any of the details of the features, or the reasons that you would choose to work with this system over one of the others. When you decide to work with this particular library, you are probably going to be curious as to what it is all about, and even why some people want to work with this while learning and working with Machine Learning.

The Scikit-Learn library is going to be the most focused on modeling data. It isn't going to take that much time to look at how to summarize the data, load the data, or manipulate the data. If you want to work through these three topics, then you would want to spend some time in the libraries of NumPy and Pandas. However, some of the features you can get through this library, and some of the different models that are available here include:

- Supervised models: This Scikit-Learn library is going to provide you with many linear models (mostly generalized) that can work well in Machine Learning. This could include some of the algorithms like a discriminate analysis, decision trees, lazy methods, the Naïve Bayes, support vector machines, and neural networks, to name a few.

- Manifold learning: These are important because they are often going to be used to help depict and summarize some of the multi-dimensional data that may seem hard to get through for a beginner.

- Parameter tuning: This is a tool that you may find useful when you want to learn more and get more out of your supervised models.

- Feature selection: This is going to be a part of the library that is going to help you see, and then identify meaningful attributes from creating a new supervised model.

- Feature extraction: This one is helpful because it is going to help you learn how to define the attributes in text data and images presented to the machine.

- Ensemble methods: You will enjoy this feature because it is going to be helpful when you combine the predictions that you have from several models of supervised learning, and then have these all come together to form a new prediction using all that information.

- A reduction in dimensionality: This is a method found in this library that is helpful when you would like to find a way to reduce the number of attributes needed in data to help with feature selection, visualization, and summarization. A good example of how this works is going to be the principal component analysis.

- Data sets: This is helpful because it is the place where you can test some of the sets of data that you have, the ones that are going to generate the right sets of data with the right properties so you can do a bit of investigating.

- Cross-validation: There are times when you will want to figure out whether a model is giving you accurate results or not. The cross-validation will help you get an estimation on how well that model is going to perform on the data that you have without it even seeing that data.

- Clustering. This is where you can group any data that doesn't have a label, such as with the K-means method that we will discuss a bit later.

These are just a few of the benefits that you are going to be able to get when it comes to working with this library. It is a strong library to use, one that is going to provide you with the results and answers that you want to many supervised Machine Learning algorithms. Without this in place, it is going to be hard to figure out how you would like to do these algorithms at all and determine if the information you get is accurate when you work with Machine Learning.

CHAPTER 6:

Why Python

Simple and Easy to Learn

The syntax and the keywords used in it are more usually in English. The quality of this language is such that it allows the programmer to concentrate on problem-solving instead of worrying about learning the syntax and how to use it. All this baggage is usually associated with several other high-level languages.

High-level Language

A high-level language means that from a developer's perspective, various internal details like memory management are abstracted from you and are then automatically taken care of by the language. This is the best high-level language for a non-programmer to learn.

Fast and Efficient to Use

Python is incredibly quick to act when it comes to the execution of actions and this is another feature that makes Python a powerful language. Any program that is written in Python can be embedded and executed just like a script within programs coded in other languages like C or C++. You can also write a simple Python script and then use it to execute any other C/C++ programs.

Open Source

Since this language is an open source, it is available free of cost. It essentially means that you can write and distribute a code written in Python. The code of Python is well-maintained so it can be constantly reused and improved upon by developed all over the world.

Interpreted

Similar to Java, even Python is an interpreted language. It means that any program that's coded in Python doesn't have to be compiled every time it must be executed. Instead, it merely needs to be compiled once and then it can be executed on various devices. For instance, if a program is written in C or C++ that's compiler based, it gets converted from the source code (into a format that humans can read) to binary code (0's and 1's of the machine language) using different flags and options that are platform specific. This binary code must then be fed into the device's memory using a linker or a loader and then it can start running. This linker, loader or compiler is an additional overhead that can be easily avoided by using a language like Python. Python doesn't compile the source code into a binary format, and it is designed in such a manner that it can be directly executed from the source code itself.

Object Oriented

As with any other modern language, even Python has an object-oriented approach towards programming. The code is organized in classes that are referred to as templates and "objects" is an example of such a class. Objects are the building blocks of an object-oriented programming language- it effectively combines data along with the methods that are used to perform any functions on this data.

Portable

It is designed in such a way that it can work on multiple platforms that require any new changes when transferring between devices. As long as you take proper care, Python is quite portable.

There are different platforms on which Python code can be used like Windows, Solaris, Macintosh, FreeBSD, VMS, Palm OS, Linux, VxWorks, and even PlayStation!

Batteries Included

When it comes to Python, it isn't merely about the speed of the execution but also about the speed of writing the code. Various inbuilt libraries and data types assist the system in completing complex operations. For all this, Python requires fewer lines of code than any other language. So, the job of the programmer is certainly made a lot easier. This feature of pre-loaded libraries is bundled up with Python and is referred to as "batteries included."

Numpy, Panda and Scikit-learn

Python offers a large inbuilt image and video library that come handy while dealing with the feature extraction phase. This feature makes Python desirable and easy to use language for Machine Learning.

The Scikit-learn package also helps in different stages of building a Machine Learning model; training the model and evaluating the system, thereby making the whole pipeline come together seamlessly. Pytorch is a good alternative for beginners.

Improved Productivity

Even though codes used in Python programming are relatively shorter, simpler, and not really much compared to other high-level programming languages such as and C++, **etc.** In the same vein, Python has well-built-in features designed to yield higher productivity. Also, it has a standard library as well as a chance to third-party modules and other source libraries. These are the unique features that make programming in Python language more yielding and efficient.

Easy Learnability

As effective as Python is, it is considerably easy to learn. This why many people prefer and find Python to be a good first language in learning programming. In fact, many programmers will recommend it over and over again for beginners. This is because Python uses simple syntax alongside shorter codes.

Easy Readability

Python programs use exact, clear, and concise instructions that are very easy to read. Those who do not even have substantial programming background will ultimately find it very easy –this is the strength of Python. Because of the cycle of edit, run and debug functions, Programs written in Python are, easy to maintain, debug, or enhance –this is readability.

Wide Support of Major Platforms

Python programming cut across works on Windows, macOS, Linux/UNIX, and other operating systems, even for small form devices. Also, it can run on devices such as remote controls, micro-controllers used in appliances, toys, embedded devices, *etc.*

Software Quality

By the readability function of Python, reusability and maintenance of the codes made it an outstanding programming language other than just the archaic scripting. The quality of the software is based on the fact that the uniformity of the codes is beyond the traditional scripting. With this, it is very easy to read it by everyone even those without foreknowledge of programming. The enhancement of coherence function in the setting of the Python also makes it of high and unique quality. The mechanism of being able to use the same codes repeatedly is a unique attribute of Python programming as well.

CHAPTER 7:

Installing Scikit -Learn

What Is Scikit-Learn?

This is going to provide your users with several supervised and unsupervised learning algorithms through a consistent Python interface. We are going to learn more about Python later in this guidebook, but it is a fantastic tool that you can use to enhance your Machine Learning, and since it is for beginners, even those who have never worked with coding in the past will be able to use it.

David Cournapeau in 2007 as a Google Summer of code project developed the Scikit-learn. This process is going to be suitable to use whether you need it commercially or academically.

Scikit-learn has been in use as a Machine Learning library inside of Python. It is going to come with numerous classifications, regression, and clustering to help you get more results. Some of the algorithms that you will get to use with this system is going to include DBSCAN, k-means, random forests, support vector machines, and gradient boosting, to name a few. And Scikit-learn was designed so that it would work well with some of the other popular libraries found on the Python code, including with SciPy and Numpy libraries.

This particular library, in particular, has been all done by Python, but some of the different formulas and algorithms that you are going to rely on to make this one work will be written with the help of Cython. If you want to make sure that the performance that you get is the best with this, you will find that the Scikit-Learn library is the one that you need to focus on. It is, especially good at building up some of the models that you need with Machine Learning. And since it is an open-sourced library, and easy to get started with, you will easily be able to open it up and start using it as soon as needed.

Understanding More About Tensor Flow

This is a framework that you can get through the Google platform, and it is used when you want to create some models in deep learning. This TensorFlow library is often going to rely on some data flow graphs that work on numerical computations. And it can stop in and make the process of Machine Learning easier than before.

You will find that working with TensorFlow makes the process of getting data, of training the models that you would like to use with Machine Learning, of making predictions, and even modifying some of the results that you see in the future so much easier. Since all of these are going to be important when it comes to Machine Learning, you can see why we want to spend some time learning TensorFlow.

TensorFlow is a library that the Brain team from Google developed to use on Machine Learning, and it is especially effective when you want to do some Machine Learning on a larger scale. TensorFlow is going to bring together algorithms that work with Deep Learning and Machine Learning, and it helps to make them more useful trough a common metaphor.

Just like what we saw when we were working on the other library, TensorFlow is going to work together well with Python, and it will ensure that you can have a front-end API that can be used when you would like to build a new application. And when you execute these applications, you will see them done in what is known as high-performance C++.

TensorFlow can be used to help out with running deep neural networks, for training, building, handwritten digit classifications, recurrent neural networks, word embedding, and even natural language processing to name a few of the neat things you will be able to do.

Both of these two libraries work well with Python, and they are going to do a remarkable job when it comes to ensuring that you are on the right track with your Machine Learning.

Both of these are going to take on a lot of different tasks, and you will need to pick out the right one based on what you would like to get done on your project.

Getting Started with Scikit-Learn

Both the Scikit-Learn and the TensorFlow library are going to need to be set up to start with Python Machine Learning. But the first one that we are going to work with setting up is the Scikit-Learn. This is a library that you can work with if you have Python 2.7 or higher on your system. If those are installed already, then you should already have things set up here. It is usually best if you are working with Machine Learning that you have one of these newer versions, so installing that can help.

Before you start with installing this library, double check and see if the SciPy and Numpy libraries are installed already —if these are not present, then you need to install them first, and then go through and install the Scikit-Learn.

The installation of these libraries may seem like it is time-consuming; it is essential and can do this with the help of pip. This pip is going to be a tool that will come along with Python, so can use the pip as soon as the system is all installed. From here, you can work with the command below to help you get the Scikit-Learn library ready to go:

From here, the installation will be able to run, and then it will complete once all of that is done. It is also possible for you to go through and use the option of conda to help install this library. The command that you will want to use to make sure that this happens is:

Conda Install Scikit-Learn

Once you notice that the installation of Scikit-learn is complete, it is time to do some importation to get it over to the Python program. This step is necessary to use the algorithms that come with it. The good news is that the command to make this happen is going to be done. You need to go to your command line and type in import sklearn.

If your command can go through without leaving behind an error message, then you know that the installation that you did was successful. After you are done with all of these steps, your scikit-learn library is on the computer, it is compatible with the Python program, and it is going to be ready to use.

Installing TensorFlow

Once you have the Scikit-Learn library put in place on your environment, it is time to start installing the TensorFlow library. When you download this one, you can get a few different APIs for other programming languages outside Python, including Java and C++, so if you need to use these, you can get a hold of them pretty easily. You can download this on a few different devices if you would like, but for this guidebook, we are going to discuss how you can install this library on a Windows computer. You can use the pip that we had from before, or Anaconda, to get this downloaded on your Windows computer.

The native pip is often the best way to get TensorFlow installed on your system, without having to worry about the virtual environment that comes with it. But one of the things that you are going to need to keep track of here is that when you install this library with a pip, there are times when this will interfere with some of the other installations of Python that are on the computer, and you need to be aware of this ahead of time.

The good thing to know here is that the only thing that you need to have up and running to make this work is a single command. And once you know this command, TensorFlow can install on your system and get it up and running. Once you can get this library installed using the pip, the user is going to see that there are some options, including the ability to choose which directory you would like to store this on.

Now, you can also choose to install the TensorFlow library on your computer with the help of Anaconda. To do this, you need first to go through and create your virtual environment. You may also want to work with a pip with this one as well. Before you start on this one, make sure that you have a

Windows system and Python 3.5 or above. Pip 3 program needs to be in place as well to help with this kind of installation. The commands you will need to get started with this one includes:

pip3 install – upgrade tensorflow

If you would like to install the GPU version of the Tensorflow program, you would need to go through and use the following command to make it happen:

pip3 install – upgrade tensorflow-gpu

This is going to ensure that you install TensorFlow on the Windows system that you are using. But another option is to install this library so that you can use it with Python and all of your other Machine Learning algorithms will include being able to install it with the help of the Anaconda package.

Pip is a program that is automatically going to get installed when you get Python on your system. But the Anaconda program isn't. This means that if you would like to make sure that TensorFlow is installed with the use of the Anaconda program, you first need to take the time to install this program. To do this, visit the website for Anaconda, download it from the website, and then find the instructions for installation from that same site.

Once you have gone through and installed the Anaconda program, you should notice that it comes with a package that is called conda. This is a good package to take some time to look at and explore a bit because it will work when you want to manage any installation packages or manage virtual environments. To get some access to this package, you need to start up the Anaconda program.

After you get to this point, you can head over to the Windows main screen and then click on the Start menu. You can choose All Programs and expand it out until you see the folder for Anaconda. You click on this prompt to launch the folder. If you need to see what details are in this package, you can run a command in the command line for "conda info." This makes it easier to see what the details for that package and the manager as well.

There are a lot of cool things that come with this Anaconda program, but one of the options that you will want to learn more about to help with Machine Learning. Anaconda can help you create an environment of Python for your own using this package. The virtual environment is going to be its isolated copy of Python, and it will have the right capabilities of maintaining all of the files that it needs, including the directories and paths. This can be helpful because it allows you to do all of these things while still working with the version of Python that you want and any of the other libraries that you want.

These virtual environments may seem like they are complicated, but it is helpful because they will provide you with a way to isolate your projects and can avoid some of the significant problems that can arise along the way. Note that this is going to be a separate environment compared to the normal Python environment that was downloaded before. This is important because you won't be able to have any effect on the regular Python environment, whether it is bad or good.

At this point, we want to do some work to help us create a virtual environment for that TensorFlow package. This can be done when we use the command of "conda create." Since we want to create a brand-new environment that we have called tensorenviron, we would need to use the formula below to help:

Conda Create -n tensorenviron

At this point, the program is going to ask you whether or not you would like to allow the process of creating the environment to continue, or if you would like to cancel the work. You will want to type in the "y," and then hit the enter key to move on. This will allow the installation to continue successfully to see the results that you want.

Once you have been able to go through this whole thing and create an environment, you will need to take a few minutes and let this environment activate it. If you do not do the activation correctly, you won't be able to use this new environment—you won't be able to get the new environment to work, either. You will be able to activate this using the command discussed earlier. From that point, you will then be able to list out the name that you would like for the environment. An excellent example of what we are talking about here and how it will work includes:

Activate tensorenviron

Now that you have been able to activate the TensorFlow environment, it is time to go ahead and make sure that the package for TensorFlow is going to be installed, too. You can do this by using the command below:

Conda Install TensorFlow

From here, the computer is going to present you with a list of all of the different packages that you can install together along with the package for TensorFlow if you would like. You will be prompted to decide if you want to install these packages or not. You can then type in the "y," and hit the enter key on the keyboard.

Once you agree to do this, the installation of this package is going to get started right away. However, notice that this particular process for installation is going to take a bit of time, so you need to wait and remain patient. However, the speed of your connection will determine the amount of time that the installation process is going to take. The progress and how far the installation have gone and yet to go will be shown on a prompt window.

After a certain time, the installation process is going to be complete, and you can then determine if the installation process was successful or not. This is pretty easy to do because you need to run the import statement with Python. The statement is going to be done from the regular terminal of Python. If you are doing this with the Anaconda prompt, you can type in "python" and hit the enter key. This is going to make sure that you end up in the terminal for Python, and from there, you can run the import statement below:

Import TensorFlow as tf

If you find that the package wasn't installed properly, you are going to end up with an error message on the screen after you do this code. If you don't see an error message, then you know that the installation of the package was successful.

CHAPTER 8:

IDE (Spyder, Jupiter)

Python Interpreter, IDLE, and the Shell

A standard installation of Python from python.org, contains documentation, licensing information and 3 main executable files which are used to develop and run python scripts.

Let's take a brief look at each of these three programs and the role each plays in python programming.

Python Interpreter

The python interpreter is the program responsible for executing the scripts you write. The interpreter converts the .py script files into bytecode instructions and then processes them according to the code written in the file.

Python IDLE

IDLE is the Python integrated development and learning environment. It contains all of the tools you will need to develop programs in Python including the shell, a text editor and debugging tools.

Depending on your python version and operating system, IDLE can be very basic or have an extensive array of options that can be setup.

For example, on Mac OS X, the text editor can be setup with several code indentation and highlighting options which can make your programs much easier to read and work with.

If the text editor in IDLE does not offer the sophistication you need, there are several aftermarket text editors which support Python script highlighting, autocomplete and other features that make script writing easier.

Python Shell

The shell is an interactive, command line driven interface to the python interpreter.

In the python shell, commands are entered at the >>> prompt. Anything that is entered at the prompt must be in proper python syntax, incorrect entries will return a syntax error like

SyntaxError: invalid syntax

When a command is entered, it is specific to that shell and has the lifetime of the shell.

For example, if you assign a variable a value such as:

>>>X=10

Then the variable is assigned an integer value of 10.

That value will be maintained until the shell is closed, restarted or the value is changed.

If another shell window is opened, the value of X will not be accessible in the new window.

When a command is entered and accepted, the code is executed. If the entered code generates a response, the response will be output to the specified device. If it does not, such as simply assigning a variable as above, then another prompt (>>>) is shown and additional commands can be entered.

This can be useful for a number of simple tasks, testing simple functions and getting a feel for how commands work.

As an example, enter the following:

```
>>>X=10
>>>Y=5
>>>print(X)
10
>>>print(Y)
5
>>>print(X+Y)
15
```

This demonstrates a couple of things.

First, we assign the two variables X and Y values.

Both variables retain their values within the shell. It also shows that the way we defined the variables was acceptable. If it is acceptable in the shell, it will be acceptable in a script.

If a command is not acceptable, it will return an error or exception.

For example, if we ask for the length of X with the following command

>>>print(len(X))

Then the following is returned:

Traceback (most recent call last):

 File "<pyshell#12>", line 1, in <module>

 print(len(X))
 TypeError: object of type 'int' has no len()

The error returned usually will provide some valuable information as to why the error occurred.

In this case, it is telling us that we assigned an integer value to X.

The len() command gives the length of a string so we are getting this error because the type of data held by the variable does not match the requirements of the function called.

If instead we had used

>>>print(len(str(X)))

2

In this case, we are using the str() command to convert the value of X into a string.

We are then using len() to get the length of that string, which is 2 characters.

This can be loosely translated into

X=12 $\rightarrow$ str(X)='12' $\rightarrow$ len('12')=2

We can continue to use the shell to explore other things like different ways to assign variable values.

For example, rather than explicitly assigning values on a per line basis, variables can be assigned as comma separated groups.

>>>X,Y = 20,12

>>>print(X,Y)

20 12

Script Editor

To create our first program, open the text editor.

To open it in a GUI OS like OS X or Windows, select File->New from the IDLE menus.

In non-GUI implementations .py files can be created in a terminal text editor like VI or VIM. Please see documentation on those programs for information on working in them.

Once a text window is open, we can simply enter our program code.

In this case, we will write a quick program for calculating the volume of a cylinder. The formula is V=(πr^2)*h where r is the radius and h are the height.

While this program will be extremely simple, and could easily be done just using the shell, it will show several fundamentally important things in Python programming.

The first step will be to import the math library.

Many functions available in python are stored in libraries. These libraries typically house functions which are grouped by task such as math.

If the proper library is not loaded when prior to making a call to that library, an error such as

Traceback (most recent call last):

  File "<pyshell#22>", line 1, in <module>

print(math.exp(2))

NameError: name 'math' is not defined

will be displayed. This error is telling you that math is not defined.

Since math is part of a Python standard library this tells you that the library was not imported prior to execution of the request for the math keyword.

In the text editor, enter the lines as follows

import math library

import math

The #is the python comment symbol. Anything between that and the end of the line is ignored by the interpreter.

One of the key advantages of Python scripting is readability so it is very important (as it is in all programing) to be diligent about commenting.

Comments will make it easier to debug your code later and will make it easier for someone else to look at your work and see how the program works.

In many cases, it also forces you to slow down and think out the programming process as you go which will lead to cleaner and better organized code.

Next, we need to set up our variables.

This can be done anywhere within a script as long as they are defined prior to calling for their value.

If a variable is called before it is defined, a 'name not defined' exception will be displayed, and program execution will halt.

assign variables

r=5 # radius

h=10 # height

V=0 # volume

While V does not need to be explicitly defined, here it is considered good practice to do so because it makes the code is easier to understand.

Next, we do the actual volume calculation.

calculate volume of a cylinder

V=(math.pi*math.pow(r,2))*h # volume=(π*r^2)*h

Next, to see the result we use the print function, which will output the result to the console.

output the result

print(V)

The complete program looks like this

import math

import math

assign variables

r=5 # radius

h=10 # height

V=0 # volume

calculate volume of a cylinder

V=(math.pi*math.pow(r,2))*h # volume=(π*r^2)*h

output the result

print(V)

You can save the program to your hard drive, let's call it cylinder.py.

Python views files ending in .py as script files so it is important to always save your scripts with the .py extension. Once we have a saved script file, we can go ahead and run it.

CHAPTER 9:

Introduction to the Main Python Libraries

Keras

Keras is a minimalist and modular neural network library that uses either Theano or TensorFlow as the backend. It allows the engineer to experiment with the data quickly and also ensures that the model predicts the results quickly. It is extremely easy to build a neural network on Keras since this library has numerous normalizers, optimizers, and activation functions.

Keras allows you to construct a sequence-based and graph-based network. This makes it easier for the engineer to implement complex architecture. The issue with Keras is that it never allows an engineer to train different models, networks, or layers in parallel. This is because it does not support the use of multiple GPUs.

Theano

If Theano is not fully developed, it is difficult for engineers to identify or work on abstraction problems. Theano is a library that is often used to define, optimize, and evaluate numerous mathematical computations regardless of its complexity. This library is often used when the data set includes multidimensional arrays. This can be done by Theano since it helps the machine spread the work across multiple GPUs. This library can be integrated with numerous libraries in Python which enables an engineer to develop complex and better models.

TensorFlow

TensorFlow is a package that has similar properties and functions like Theano. It is an open source package that is used to perform numerical computations.

The Google Intelligence Organization developed this library, and an engineer can use the different functions and tools in this package to distribute the functions being performed by the model between different GPUs. TensorFlow is often used as the backend when you build a neural network in Python using Keras.

Scikit-Learn

Scikit-learn is an open source Python library. This library is often used to implement different visualization, Machine Learning, preprocessing, and cross-validation algorithms. This is often done using a unified interface.

The functions and features in this package can be used for both data mining and data analysis. These functions include support vector machines, clustering, random forests, gradient boosting, classification, regression, and k-means algorithms.

ERIC CHAMBERLIN

CHAPTER 10:

Introduction to Bias and Variance

The aim of Machine Learning models is to learn from training data. Once the model is trained, it should have a framework of knowledge relating to that domain, so when given the input data (X), it should be able to predict with a high probability the label (Y), a poor model will have a high prediction error rate. A poor model with a high error prediction rate will generally have a problem in one of three areas, Bias which typically is a generalization error and relates to the model underfitting the training data.

Variance which has an excessive sensitivity to small variations in the training data, will cause the model to overfit on the training data. Irreducible error is usually caused by the data itself, where the noisiness of the data makes it hard to detect patterns and carry out classifications.

Cleaning up the data or removing outliers so patterns in the data can reveal themselves can help prevent irreducible errors.

Therefore, to optimize the model the aim should be to create a finely-tuned counterbalance between bias and variance, which is called the bias–variance trade-off. If we were to reduce the model's complexity, it reduces its variance, but it will increase its bias. Conversely, if we were to increase the model's complexity, it reduces its bias but will increase its variance.

CHAPTER 11:

Evaluating the error in the Regression models (RMSE, MAE, R2)

Regression, a word that many people hear and immediately fear due to its complexity, is a statistical process that people use in order to estimate and define relationships between and among various variables. Regression as a whole refers to multiple techniques that allow us to model the relationship between a dependent variable and one or multiple independent variables, known as predictors. Regression analysis is very useful for helping us understand how the criterion variable, or the dependent variable as it is commonly known, is affected and changes whenever some independent variable changes, while the other independent variables, if any, remain fixed. Regression analysis is also used to help estimate the conditional expectation of the criterion variable given the predictors, so we know what the criterion variable's value the predictors will be once they are fixed. However, there are also those that use regression analysis to focus on some location parameters of the dependent variable's distribution in relation to the independent variables.

Notably, due to the characteristics of regression analysis, where the data points fluctuate depending on what is being controlled for, the outputs tend to be in a continuous form rather than in a discrete form, matching the changes in real – time.

Regression Analysis

Regression is a supervised Machine Learning algorithm. In regression, given an input, when the output of the model is a numeric value, this means that we are going to learn a numeric algorithm not a class, $C(x) \in \{0, 1\}$. Regression is exploited to derive equations that best describe the data. The goal is then to utilize this model to generate estimations. The common and the simplest way of regression is the linear regression. The linear regression is preferred to find a predictive function when we have a correlation coefficient indicates that the data can predict upcoming events. Moreover, if a scatter plot of data seems to be a straight line, the linear regression is also preferred.

Linear regression is a method to tell how two variables are related. Recalling from algebra, the famous line equation is $y = mx + b$. This is the famous line equation from elementary algebra. However, we can describe the analogy from the Machine Learning and linear regression concepts perspective. We have: y as a variable that is dependent, a function of, another variable, x as an independent variable, m is the slope and b is the Y-intercept. We need first, to find the linear regression equation, to decide how the two variables, x and y, are related. In a dataset, we normally have a list of values in columns format, which can be filled as the x and y values or w and q as used in the following series of equations.

Note, before proceeding to the regression equation: when we say that there is a relationship between two variables, this does not necessarily mean that one is the cause of the other. Therefore, it is recommended to firstly, generate a scatter graph in order to decide if the data somehow makes a line prior to calculate the equation of the linear regression.

The Equation of the Linear Regression

The formula of the linear regression equation is:

$$Q = mW + b \quad (3.1)$$

Which is the famous linear equation formula. The slope, m and the intercept, b are calculated form the following two equations, respectively:

$$m = \frac{n\sum wq - \left(\sum w \cdot \sum q\right)}{n\sum w^2 - \left(\sum w\right)^2} \quad (3.2)$$

$$b = \frac{\left(\sum q \cdot \sum w^2\right) - \left(\sum w \cdot \sum wq\right)}{n\sum w^2 - \left(\sum w\right)^2} \quad (3.3)$$

Where, n is the number of records. Now, to understand how this work, we suppose that we have the following data, shown in the table 3.1 below:

W	Q
45	91
23	67
27	81
41	70
49	83
60	77

Table 3-1 Age and Glucose relationship

The dataset above relates two attributes; X: is the age and Y: is the Glucose level. To make the evaluation easier, we make the following table 3.2:

W	Q	WQ	W_2	Q_2
45	91	4095	2025	8281
23	67	1541	529	4489
27	81	2187	729	6561

41 70 2870 1681 4900

49 83 4067 2401 6889

60 77 4620 3600 5929

$\sum$ 245 469 19380 10965 37049

Table 3-2 Age and Glucose relationship extended

Our mission now is to use the values in the table above to calculate the slope and the intercept from equations (2) and (3), respectively. The values of m and b are found to be:

$$m = 0.2385$$

$$b = 68.428$$

Now we insert these values in the linear regression equation, which represented as follows: $y = 0.2385X + 68.43$ (3.4)

Equation (4) is known as the linear regression equation. The values 0.2385 and 68.43 are called regression weights. The calculation process of these weights is known as regression. Once we calculated the weights, we can utilize the regression learning algorithms to make new predictions given an unseen values/dataset. This can be easily achieved by multiplying the inputs by the regression weights and then adding them together to get a prediction. To grasp what have been done, you may export this table into an excel sheet, then generate the scatter plot of dataset in table 3.1. Then, the linear equation is plotted. The resulted plot is as follows, in 3.1:

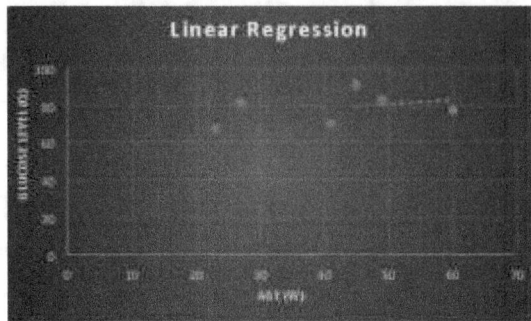

Figure 3.1 The scatter data and the linear regression equation plot

The line generated by this equation is called: the trend line. An online linear regression calculator is available on the link in the lower margin [8].

Testing with R^2 correlation:

Correlation is an estimate of how close the trend line to fit the data points that you have in your dataset. In other words, an estimation of the success of the model. It can be somehow estimated by eye from the scatter plot, as we mentioned before, but to make an exact decision we utilize the correlation coefficient; named: R^2. Normally, the closer R^2 is to 1, the better the line fits the data points. If R^2 is far from 1, the line definitely, will not fit the data. The correlation factor equation is:

$$R^2 = \frac{(n\sum wq - \sum w \sum q)^2}{(n\sum w^2 - (\sum w)^2)(n\sum q^2 - (\sum q_i)^2)} \quad [3.5]$$

Utilizing this equation helps engineer or data scientist to make an exact expectation of the accuracy of applying the regression algorithm.

ERIC CHAMBERLIN

CHAPTER 12:

Supervised Learning

In the supervised approach to Machine Learning, researchers first construct a mathematical model of a data set which includes the expected inputs and the required outputs. The data this produces is called training data and consists of sets of training examples (input and desired output). Each of these training examples is comprised of one or more inputs, along with the desired output – the supervisory signal. In semi-supervised learning, some of the desired output values are missing from the training examples.

Through iteration, that is, running the training data through the learning algorithm repeatedly, the learning algorithm develops a function to match the desired outputs from the inputs of the training data. During the iteration, this function is optimized by the learning algorithm. When this system is deemed ready, new data sets are introduced that are missing the desired outputs – these are known as the testing sets. At this point, errors or omission in the training data may become more obvious and the process can be repeated with new or more accurate output requirements. An algorithm that successfully modifies itself to improve the accuracy of its predictions or outputs can be said to have successfully learned to perform a task.

Supervised and semi-supervised learning algorithms include two classes of data handling — classification and regression. When outputs are limited by a constrained set of possible values, classification learning algorithms are employed. But when the outputs can be returned as a numerical value in a range of possible values, regression learning algorithms are the best fit.

Finally, there is similarity learning. While closely related to regression and classification learning, the goal of similarity learning is to examine data sets and determine how similar or different the information sets are. Similarity learning can be used in tasks such as ranking, recommendation systems (Netflix recommended anyone?), visual identity tracking, facial recognition/verification, and speaker (audio) verification.

Supervised Learning Algorithms

Classification

Classification involves discovering the inherent groupings of present in a set of data. The categorization of customers based upon their purchasing behaviors is an example of classification. Characterization of emails as either spam or non-spam is another. Other examples include the bull and bear cycle in property market, characterization of student grades and prediction of employee churn

Let's look at some of the classification algorithms for Machine Learning:

Logistic Regression

A logistic regression algorithm uses a logistic function to make predictions valued between 0 and This is an indication that these predictions can be interpreted to be class probabilities. Due to the linear nature of these models, they work well when you have linearly separable classes, meaning that a single decision surface can be used for separating the classes.

Advantages of this algorithm are that the outputs will have a proper probabilistic interpretation, and that it is possible to regularize the algorithm (by penalizing the coefficients with tunable penalty strength) so as to avoid the problem of overfitting.

However, linear regression does not perform well when you have nonlinear or multiple decision boundaries. Also, they are not good for capturing complex relationships.

Classification Tree (Ensembles)

They are good for classification problems, and they work in the same way as regression trees. Practically, they perform very well.

They are also scalable, robust to outliers and naturally model the nonlinear decision boundaries due to their hierarchical structure.

However, individual trees are vulnerable to over fitting which can be solved by use of the ensemble methods.

Deep Learning

Deep learning can be categorized to be as part of a classification problem. A good example is image classification. A deep learning algorithm will give you a very nice performance when you are classifying text, audio and image data.

However, deep neural networks require a huge training data set, and that is why it is a general-purpose algorithm.

Support Vector Machines (SVM)

SVMs use kernels for the purpose of calculating the distance between any two observations. The algorithm looks for a decision boundary which maximizes the distance between the closest members of separate classes.

SVMs can be used for modeling nonlinear decision boundaries, and they provide many kernels from which to choose. They are not prone to overfitting, especially in cases in which you have a high-dimensional space.

SVM is a memory intensive algorithm, however, and the importance of selecting the right kernel makes it hard to tune the model. This algorithm is not suitable for use with larger data sets.

Naïve Bayes

This algorithm works based on counting and conditional probability. The model is simply a probability table which is updated depending on training data.

For you to make a prediction, you observe the class probabilities in the probability table based on the feature values. It was given the name naïve because of its conditional independence assumption which is a rare occurrence in real world.

Naïve Bayes models are easy to implement and offer a very good performance. They scale very well with your dataset.

ERIC CHAMBERLIN

CHAPTER 13:

Linear Regression

Linear regression is probably the most well-known of all the algorithms associated with Machine Learning. The fundamental concept of this algorithm is to find the path that best models the linear trend, or in other words, finding the line that best fits the problem. It assumes that a linear relationship exists between the different input variables.

When there is only one input variable (x), the method used is called a simple linear regression but if there are multiple input variables, the method is referred to as multiple linear regression.

Linear regression is one of the most popular types of predictive analysis. Linear regression involves the following two things:

- Do the predictor variables forecast the results of an outcome variable accurately?

- Which particular variable are key predictors of the final variable, and in what standard does it impact the outcome variable?

- Naming variables
- Functions of the regression analysis
- Trend Forecasting
- Determine the strength of predictors
- Predict an effect
- Breaking down regression

There are two basic states of regression-linear and multiple regression. Although there are different methods for complex data and analysis. Linear regression contains an independent variable to help forecast the outcome of a dependent variable. On the other hand, multiple regression has two or more independent variables to assist in predicting a result. Regression is very useful to financial and investment institutions because it is used to predict the sales of a particular product or company based on the previous sales and GDP growth among many other factors. The capital pricing model is one of the most common regression models applied in the finance. The example below describes formulae used in the linear and multiple regression.

```
Linear Regression: Y = a + bX + u
Multiple Regression: Y = a + b1X1 + b2X2 + b3X3 + ... + btXt + u
In this case:
Y = variable which you want to predict (dependent variable)
X = variable which you are using to predict Y (independent variable)
a = the intercept
b = the slope
u = regression residual
```

Choosing the best regression model

Selecting the right linear regression model can be very hard and confusing. Trying to model it with a sample data cannot make it easier.

This section reviews some of the most popular statistical methods which one can use to choose models, challenges that you might come across, and lists some practical advice to use to select the correct regression model.

It always begins with a researcher who would like to expand the relationship between the response variable and predictors. The research team that is accorded with the responsibility to perform investigation essentially measures a lot of variables but only has a few in the model.

The analysts will make efforts to reduce the variables that are different and apply the ones which have an accurate relationship. As time moves on, the analysts continue to add more models.

Statistical Methods Used to Find the Best Regression Model

If you want a great model in regression, then it is important to take into consideration the type of variables which you want to test as well as other variables which can affect the response.

Modified R-squared and Predicted R-squared.

Your model should have a higher modified and predicted R-squared values. The statistics are shown below help eliminate critical issues which revolve around R-squared.

• The adjusted R squared increases once a new term improves the model.

• Predicted R-squared belongs to the cross-validation that helps define the manner in which your model can generalize remaining data sets.

P-values for the Predictors

When it comes to regression, a low value of P denotes statistically significant terms. The term "Reducing the model" refers to the process of factoring in all candidate predictors contained in a model.

Stepwise regression

This is an automated technique which can select important predictors found in the exploratory stages of creating a model.

Real World Challenges

There are different statistical approaches for choosing the best model. However, complications still exist.

- The best model happens when the variables are measured by the study.

- The sample data could be unusual because of the type of data collection method. A false positive and false negative process happens when you handle samples.

- If you deal with enough models, you'll get variables that are significant but only correlated by chance.

- P-values can be different depending on the specific terms found in the model.

- Studies have discovered that the best subset regression and stepwise regression can't select the correct model.

Finding the correct Regression Model

Theory

Perform research done by other experts and reference it into your model. It is important that before you start regression analysis, you should develop ideas about the most significant variables. Developing something based on outcome from other people eases the process of collecting data.

Complexity

You may think that complex problems need a complex model. Well, that is not the case because studies show that even a simple model can provide an accurate prediction. Once there is a model with the same explanatory potential, the simplest model is likely to be a perfect choice. You just need to start with a simple model as you slowly advance the complexity of the model.

How to Calculate the Accuracy of the Predictive Model?

There are different ways in which you can compute the accuracy of your model. Some of these methods include:

You divide the dataset into a test and training data set. Next, build the model based on the training set and apply the test set as a holdout sample to measure your trained model with the test data.

The next thing to do is to compare the predicted values using actual values by computing the error by using measures like the "Mean Absolute Percent Error" (MAPE). If your MAPE is less than 10%, then you have a great model.

2. Another method is to calculate the "Confusion Matrix" to the computer False Positive Rate and False Negative Rate.

These measures will allow a person to choose whether to accept the model or not. If you consider the cost of the errors, it becomes a critical stage of your decision whether to reject or accept the model.

3. Computing Receiver Operating Characteristic Curve (ROC) or the Lift Chart or Area under the curve (AUC) are other methods that you can use to decide on whether to reject or to accept a model.

ERIC CHAMBERLIN

CHAPTER 14:

Random Forests -Theory

Bias Variance Decomposition The error of model ϕL generalization is the anticipated error of prediction when you look at the loss function L

Err(ϕL)=EXY{$L(Y,\phi L(x))$}

The expected error of prediction of ϕL at X=x can be expressed as $Err(\phi_L(x)) = E_{Y|X=x}[L(Y,\phi_L(x))]$

When you look at regression, the loss of error squared, the result of error predicted is the anticipated disintegration of variance, a bias that comprises a useful framework for diagnosing the model's prediction error. When you get into the classifications zero-one, it is hard to obtain the same decomposition. The variance and bias concepts transpose in different ways into classification, providing frameworks that are comparable to the study of prediction classifiers error.

Regression When you look at regression, and you assume L as the squared error loss, the model of prediction error ϕL at point X=x can be rephrased according to Bayes model ϕB:

$$\text{Err}\{\varphi_L(x)\}$$

$$= E_{Y|X=x}\{(Y - \varphi_L(x))^2\}$$
$$= E_{Y|X=x}\{(Y - \varphi_B(x) + \varphi_B(x) - \varphi_L(x))^2\}$$
$$= E_{Y|X=x}\{(Y - \varphi_B(x))^2\} + E_{Y|X=x}\{(\varphi_B(x) - \varphi_L(x))^2\}$$
$$\hookrightarrow + E_{Y|X=x}\{2(Y - \varphi_B(x))(\varphi_B(x) - \varphi_L(x))\}$$
$$= E_{Y|X=x}\{(Y - \varphi_B(x))^2\} + E_{Y|X=x}\{(\varphi_B(x) - \varphi_L(x))^2\}$$
$$= \text{Err}\{\varphi_B(x)\} + (\varphi_B(x) - \varphi_L(x))^2$$

By Bayes model regression, $E_{Y|X=x}\{Y-\varphi_B(x)\} \cdot E_{Y|X=x}\{Y-\varphi_B(x)\} = 0$. The last expression in the equation tallies with the irreducible error at X=x the 2nd term in the variation of ϕL taken from Bayes model. If the distance is greater from the Bayes model. The error enlarges as the sub-suitable model grows enormous.

If there is an assumption that the learning set L is a random variable and there is a deterministic learning algorithm, inconsistencies with L in the Bayes model is articulated in projecting $EL\{\phi L(x)\}$ above the proficient models by understanding the feasible sets of N:

$$E_L\{(\varphi_B(x) - \varphi_L(x))^2\}$$
$$= E_L\{(\varphi_B(x) - E_L\{\varphi_L(x)\} + E_L\{\varphi_L(x)\} - \varphi_L(x))^2\}$$
$$= E_L\{(\varphi_B(x) - E_L\{\varphi_L(x)\})^2\} + E_L\{(E_L\{\varphi_L(x)\} - \varphi_L(x))^2\}$$
$$\hookrightarrow + E_L\{2(\varphi_B(x) - E_L\{\varphi_L(x)\})(E_L\{\varphi_L(x)\} - \varphi_L(x))\}$$
$$= E_L\{(\varphi_B(x) - E_L\{\varphi_L(x)\})^2\} + E_L\{(E_L\{\varphi_L(x)\} - \varphi_L(x))^2\}$$
$$= (\varphi_B(x) - E_L\{\varphi_L(x)\})^2 + E_L\{(E_L\{\varphi_L(x)\} - \varphi_L(x))^2\} \quad (4.4)$$

Since $E_L\{\varphi_B(x) \cdot E_L\{\varphi_L(x)\} \cdot E_L\{\varphi_L(x)\}\} = 0$ in conclusion, the generalization error expected decomposes additively in the theory below.

Theorem Bias variance decomposition is from loss error squared; the anticipated generalization error $E_c\{Err\{\varphi_c(x)\}\}$ at $X=x$ is

$$E_c\{Err\{\varphi_c(x)\}\} = noise(x) + bias^2(x) + var(x),$$

where

$$noise(x) = Err\{\varphi_B(x)\},$$
$$bias^2(x) = \{\varphi_B(x) - E_c\{\varphi_c(x)\}\}^2,$$
$$var(x) = E_c\{\{E_c\{\varphi_c(x)\} - \varphi_c(x)\}^2\}.$$

This bias-variance-decomposition of the error of generalization was discussed in neural networks in 1992. The idiom noise is a lingering error. The algorithm is free of the learning set. It also provides a theoretical lower bound on the generalization error. Bias2 makes a measure of the discrepancy between the Bayes model projection and an average projection. var Computes other variabilities of the X=x variations over the models.

How to Interpret Random Forests

A response variable prediction based on prediction variables that are set is an important expedition in science. The aim is to make accurate response prediction; but to accurately single out predictor variables crucial in creating projections, like, for instance, is to understand the underlying process. Since they are used in many problem scenarios, and their accuracy to build models that are accurate, and in the provision of the importance measures, the major data analysis tool that I used successfully, in different scenarios is the random forests.

Despite the wide applications, there are only a few works that have looked into the algorithms theoretical and statistical mechanisms and properties.

Variable importance When you factor in single-decision trees, the measure of importance of the variables Xj was as

$$\text{Imp}(X_j) = \sum_{t \in \varphi} \Delta I(\tilde{s}_t^j, t),$$

Where $\tilde{s}_t^j$ is the understudy split for s*t*, which is a split closely defined on variable Xj that mirrors the split s*t* interpreted in t node? Surrogate splits were used to account for masking-effects. However, if Xj2 another tree is grown in place of the removal of Xj1, then the second split may occur in the tree and split with the results may relatively be as great as the first tree. When this happens, then the relevant measure detects the Xj2 importance.

Asymptotic analysis A tree that is totally random and developed is a decision tree with t node being separated by the use of a variable Xj that was selected in a consistent erratic manner among the neglected parent-nodes t, that split to [Xj] sub trees.

In these trees, the depth is similar to all leaves*p* and those at s*t* of grown tree is bijection with X of the feasible joint configuration of a variable. An instance is, all variable inputs are in binary, the forthcoming of the tree will have 2p leaves.

Non-totally randomized trees Built at random, the trees are not related to those extremely randomized trees or random forests. To comprehend the algorithms that are computed, take an alternative of node t of randomized trees, drawn equally at random 1≤K≤p variables. Choose one that utilizes. Like previously, t is split to several sub-trees like the cardinality of the variable that is chosen. Know that, K=1, it aggregates to the construction of classical trees that are single in a way that is deterministic.

ERIC CHAMBERLIN

CHAPTER 15:

Evaluation Metrics and Classification Models

Model Evaluation

It is always good to evaluate your model to determine whether it will predict the target correctly in the cases of both new and future data. The target values for your future data are unknown, hence you should use the data you have and its corresponding target values to determine the accuracy metric of your model.

The assessment should be used as a proxy for predictive accuracy on your future data.

To evaluate a model correctly, hold the data set whose target values are known. This should be obtained from the data source. It is not advisable for you to use the data that was used to train a Machine Learning model to test its predictive accuracy.

This will only reward models that can "remember" training data rather than drawing generalizations from it.

Once you have trained a Machine Learning model, the held-out observations whose target values are known should be send to the model. Then compare the results you get from the model with the target values or the known values.

If you get the difference between the two, you will be able to tell how accurate your Machine Learning model is. Finally, compute a summary metric telling you how true the predicted and the true values match.

Preventing Overfitting

When you are creating and training your Machine Learning model, your goal should be to choose the model that makes the best predictions, which is the model displaying the best settings.

There is a danger in choosing a model's parameter settings that give the best "predictive" performance on evaluation data. You may end up "overfitting" your model.

Overfitting normally occurs when a model has memorized the patterns occurring in training and evaluation data sources, but it has failed to generalize the patterns in data. An overfitted model will perform well during evaluations, but it is unable to make accurate predictions on any unseen data.

To avoid an overfitted model, preserve some data to use in validating the performance of your Machine Learning model.

You can choose to use 60% of your data for training, 20% of it for evaluation, and the remaining 20% for validation.

Once you have chosen the model parameters for the evaluation data, you can run a second evaluation using the validation data and see how well your Machine Learning model performs. If the test meets your expectations using your validation data, it is not overfitted.

Cross-Validation

Cross-validation refers to the process of evaluating Machine Learning models in which several Machine Learning models are trained on the subsets of the available input data, then evaluating them on complementary subset of the data. Cross-validation can be used to detect overfitting.

The k-fold cross validation is a nice method for cross-validation. In this method, the input data is split into k subsets of data, which are also known as *folds*. A Machine Learning model is then trained on all except one of the data sets; that is, the training is done with *k-1* datasets.

The evaluation of the model is then done using the subset that was not used for training. The training process is then repeated several times, using a different dataset for evaluation each time. This means the process is repeated k times.

Confidence Interval

This is a good metric for assessing the reliability of a statistical estimate. A wide confidence interval is an indication you have a poor model. If the confidence interval doesn't change after modifying the model, it means your data is very noisy.

Confusion Matrix

This is a technique used to evaluate the prediction power of a model employing a clustering algorithm. It is an $N * N$ matrix, in which N represents the cluster number.

The matrix should be designed as follows:

The element contained in cell (i, j) shows the number of the observations in the data set for training that belongs to ith cluster and have been assigned to the cluster j.

After the numbers have been changed into proportions, the matrices are referred to as "contingency tables".

An observation that has been assigned incorrectly is referred to as a "false positive" or a "false negative" A higher number of observations along the diagonal of a confusion matrix indicates the model is more accurate when making predictions.

CHAPTER 16:

Unsupervised Learning

Unsupervised Learning Algorithms

In unsupervised learning, algorithms are simply given large data sets containing only inputs. Their goal is to find structure in the data, grouped, or clustered data points that can be compared to new data sets. Unsupervised learning algorithms learn from data that has no labels and has not been organized or classified before being submitted. Instead of attempting to produce a required output prompted by supervisory systems, these algorithms attempt to find commonalities in the inputs they receive, which they then apply to new data sets. They react when these commonalities are found, missing, or broken in each new data set. Unsupervised learning algorithms are used in diverse fields including density estimation in statistics and the summarizing and explanation of data features. This type of learning can also be useful in fraud detection, where the goal is to find anomalies in input data.

Cluster analysis is when unsupervised learning algorithms break down a set of observations about data in clusters (subsets) so that the information within each cluster is similar based on one or more predefined criteria. Information drawn from other clusters will be internally similar, while dissimilar from each other. There are different approaches to data clustering, which are derived from making alternative assumptions about the structure of the data.

The training data set for unsupervised learning algorithms contains input data (X) only. No output data (Y) is given.

The name **unsupervised** comes from the fact that there is no "teacher" (output); and the correct answers are not given known.

The goal of unsupervised learning is to model the underlying distribution or structure of the data and to learn more from the data. The algorithm is tasked with discovering the underlying data structure on its own.

Clustering

In clustering problems, our aim is to discover the inherent groupings of our data. For example, groupings of customers based upon their purchasing behaviors. Other applications of clustering include the grouping of related items in e-commerce, and various social network analyses.

The product of a cluster in algorithm is usually a data visualization enabling the user to see and evaluate the results.

Examples of clustering algorithms include k-Means k-Medians, Expectation Maximization (EM) and Hierarchical Clustering.

In clustering, our goal is to map the data into different groups known as clusters. Related data will be placed in the same cluster, while no different data will appear in the same cluster.

Dimensionality Reduction

Just like the clustering algorithms, the dimensionality reduction algorithms work to identify the underlying structure of a dataset.

Dimensionality Reduction algorithms are further divided into the following:

Feature Selection

Feature Extraction

The term "dimensionality" in Machine Learning denotes the number of features in a dataset. If the number of features happens to be large compared to the number of observations in the dataset, some of learning algorithms will find it tough to train effective models. This is what is referred to as "Curse of Dimensionality".

Feature Selection helps in filtering redundant or irrelevant features from your dataset.

The difference between feature selection and feature extraction is that in feature selection, a subset of original features is kept while in feature extraction, brand new features are created.

In dimensionality reduction, the goal is to reduce the number of features which are under consideration, and each feature is a dimension which represents the objects.

Reinforce Learning Algorithms

The goal of Reinforce Learning Algorithms is a decision model which, given a certain combination of inputs (situation) will produce a desirable output (response). The desired outputs (responses) are not given for training, only the inputs (situation), but reinforcements are given based upon the desirability of the decision (response).

The learning process involves the discovery of the best decision, which is the one producing the maximum reward.

A good example of reinforced learning is a child's process of learning to walk. The child must watch others who are walking and try to imitate them. He or she will realize that in order to walk, he must first stand up. She will stagger and slip, but still be determined to stand. The next task will be to stand unassisted. The child must be able to release his or her grasp on supports. Finally, he or she will attempt to walk decide which foot to start with, learn to balance the body weight, **etc.**

The mathematical framework for obtaining a solution to reinforced learning problems is known as the Markov Decision Process.

The process can be defined as follows:

Set of states, S

Set of actions, A

Reward function, R

Policy, π

Value, V

An action (A) is required in order for us to transition from the start state to the end state (S). We will earn a reward (R) for each action taken. Note that we can get either positive or negative rewards for our actions. The actions taken define the policy (π) and the rewards obtained define our value (V). Our goal is to maximize the reward by selecting the right policy.

The travelling salesman problem is a good example to which reinforced learning can be applied. The goal is to move from the start point to the end point at the lowest cost possible.

Graphically, this is represented in the form of nodes and edges, and the edges have values on them which indicate the cost of moving from one point to another. In this case, the value is the total cumulative reward (accumulated during the progression from node to node) during the execution of a policy.

In both reinforced and supervised learning, there is mapping from the inputs to the outputs. However, reinforced learning algorithms have a reward which provides feedback to the learning agent whereas, supervised learning has an external supervisor that share the knowledge with the agent to accomplish the task.

In unsupervised learning, there is no mapping from inputs to the outputs. The goal in unsupervised learning is to identify the underlying pattern or trend in a dataset.

CHAPTER 17:

Deep learning

Deep learning is a subfield of Machine Learning involving algorithms that are inspired by the function and structure of the brain known as artificial neural networks. It teaches computers to do what is natural to humans, that is, learn by example. It is the technology behind the concept of the driverless car.

Both Neural Networks and Deep Learning are going to give you the best solution to any problem that you may come up against when you are working with image, speech and natural language recognition and processing.

Even without a background in computer science, one can understand what the term 'Machine Learning is.' Basically, it is a machine that learns from data. As long as the machine has the right data input there is a huge number of problems that it can solve without any human interference. As long as the machine is given the correct training data and the right algorithms, it can perform the necessary functions and continue to learn from them for an indefinite period of time.

The primary tools at the heart of deep learning are the input data and algorithms. Without the correct data, it is not possible for deep learning to take place. For years, machines have functioned without algorithms, but these machines are programmed to perform certain functions without change (think vending machines) which means the program it started out with will not adapt over time. It will still perform the same actions over and over again regardless of the environment that surrounds it.

But for those who don't fully grasp computer science concepts, the thought of deep learning might instill fear instead of excitement. After all, in the past few decades, the subject has been approached with a lot of skepticism and doubt. Movies have portrayed power hungry machines bent on taking over the world, and news reports about every self-functioning machine failure have been exploited to the highest level. It leads some people to believe that machines capable of learning are more of a threat to humanity than a help. So, what exactly is this kind of technology used for and do we really have anything to worry about?

Classification

Deep learning machines have extremely comprehensive databases and sophisticated networks that allow for easy classification of many different forms of data. We might assume that looking at a picture and identifying its contents is pretty basic stuff. To the human eye, images can be classified in a fraction of a second but to a machine, which only sees things in terms of math, they contain many different elements that must first be sorted out.

Deep learning, however, makes it possible for machines to classify any type of data including video, speech, audio, or handwriting and analyze it to come up with a conclusion that would be similar to that of most humans.

Imagine a computer system that can automatically create a record of the number of vehicles that pass through a certain point on a public road during a set time frame. The steps needed for this to happen are immense. Not only would it have to hold a huge database of different types of cars, their shapes, and sizes but it must also capable of processing the data and analyzing it to come up with an acceptable answer.

Comparing the data, it receives through its sensors to the data it has stored in the database, it can classify the answer with a pretty high level of accuracy. While humans could easily identify cars by make and model, the idea of having a human standing on a street corner counting and labeling cars would virtually be impossible to achieve. Even if someone could position themselves to count, humans get tired and need to have frequent breaks. They cannot function continuously without stopping. The level of accuracy would be much lower. Yet, automobile manufacturers, government agencies, and other industries could find the information extremely valuable in making decisions for their business.

But deep learning goes even further than this. While the system may already be programmed with a massive database, as the machine operates it will learn even more and increase its knowledge from its experiences. By being programmed to train itself, continuous human interaction is not necessary. The machine will learn from its mistakes in much the same way as humans do.

Pattern recognition

Pattern recognition is probably the oldest form of Machine Learning but is also the most fundamental. As of 2015, pattern recognition was one of the most popular areas of interest in research labs around the globe. By giving a machine the ability to recognize a character or some other object, the potential for Machine Learning increased exponentially.

The ability of a machine to recognize handwritten numbers and letters opens the door to a myriad of uses. This ability has been successful in providing insights into the complex movements of the environment, weather changes, and even in the world of finance. But deep learning involves more than just identifying similar characteristics and differences in images. Pattern recognition allows them to draw their own conclusions in regard to the images or videos they are analyzing and tagging them appropriately. Every time they perform this type of analysis, the better it will become at identifying similar situations and unusual anomalies that could affect the outcome.

There are many uses for pattern recognition in many areas. It can be used to expand the 'Internet of Things' by collecting data from any device that is connected to the internet. Cities will use it to understand how people navigate through their streets, urban planners can make better decisions about the location of physical infrastructures and even in the area of conservation, it can be helpful. Instead of using manpower to go out and count trees, drones can be deployed to analyze the number of trees and their health in any given area.

ERIC CHAMBERLIN

CHAPTER 18:

Logistic Regression-Theory

The standard practice is to use the least square method, where the idea is to shorten the distance between the line and the training data. Basically, the system is looking for a line that is "nearest" to all the input data.

In regression, the relationships between variables are modeled. Regression algorithms should be used for problems in which the response variable is continuous or numeric. However, in classification algorithms, the response variables are made up of data group into classes (usually, two classes).

A regression algorithm is a good predictor of a value such as the price of a product (based upon related input variables).

The learning process is centered on a training dataset with labeled inputs and the numeric target variable. The model is refined iteratively through a process in which a model is generated, tested against the data set for accuracy, adjusted generating a new model....

Regression algorithms are heavily applied in statistical Machine Learning. Some examples are the house valuation vs the selling price and predictive returns vs realized returns in unit trusts.

More information will be shared the following chapters.

To conclude, in supervised learning, there is an external supervisor who has knowledge about the environment and shares it with the agent so as to accomplish the task.

You can also work with an algorithm that is known as a regression analysis. This is a type that will have you investigate what type of relationship that shows up between your predictor variables and your dependent variables. You will often see that this is a great technique to work on when you want to see if there is a causal relationship between the forecasting, the time-series modeling you have, and your variables. The point of working with this algorithm is designed to fit everything onto a line, or a curve, as much as possible, to help you see if there are any common factors that show up.

There are many companies who will use the regression algorithm to help them make great predictions that will increase their profits. You will be able to use it to come up with a great estimation of the sales growth for the company while still basing it on how the economic conditions in the market are doing right at this moment.

The great thing about this is that you can add in any information that you would like to use. You can add in information about the past and the current economy to this particular algorithm, such as your past and current economic information, and then this gives you an idea of how the growth will go in the future. Of course, you do need to have the right information about the company to make this happen.

For example, if you use the regression algorithm and find that your company is growing at the same rate as what other industries are doing in the economy, you would then be able to use this information to help make predictions for how your company will do in the future if the economy does end up changing.

When it comes to working with regression algorithms, you will easily see the relationship that is there between the independent variables and the dependent variables. This algorithm is also there to show what kind of impact will show up if you try to add in or change some of the variables that are in your set of data.

However, there are some shortcomings that come with the regression algorithm. The biggest one is that you will not be able to use this algorithm to help you with some classification problems. The reason that this doesn't work is that it will try too hard to overfit the data in many cases. So, any time that you are trying to add in some different constraints to this, the whole process will be really tedious for you to get done.

As you can see, there are a lot of algorithms that you can use when it comes to working on supervised Machine Learning. Supervised Machine Learning is a great way to help you make a program that can do the learning on its own, and the type of algorithm that you will use will depend on the project that you want to complete. The different algorithms are all going to have a ton of applications, which are meant to be there to help you look through all the data that you have (no matter how much you have), make predictions, and do some of the other tasks that you may need to complete when you are using them to help with Machine Learning.

CHAPTER 19:

KNN -theory

This is a type of algorithm that you can use with supervised Machine Learning is the KNN, or the k-nearest neighbors, algorithm. When you use this algorithm, you will use it to search throughout all of the data that you have for k most similar examples of whatever data instance you are trying to work on. Once you are successful with this, the KNN algorithm is then able to look through it all and summarize the results before it uses these results to make predictions for that instance.

When you use the KNN algorithm model, you can use this as a way to be competitive in your learning. This works because there is some competition between the different elements in the various models so that it is successful in making predictions.

This one does work a little bit different compared to the other options we have talked about above. It is sometimes seen as a lazier learning process because it is not going to create any models for you until you ask it for a brand-new prediction. This is sometimes a good thing depending on the case because it can ensure that the data you are working with is always relevant to the task that you want it for.

There are many benefits that come with using the KNN algorithm. When you pick out this algorithm, you can cut through the noise that is inside your data set. This is because it will rely on a competitive method to sort through the data that you see as desirable. The KNN algorithm is great at handling large amounts of data at the same time, helping you out if you have huge sets of data that need to be gone through.

The biggest issue that comes with using this particular algorithm is that it does have a high computational cost, especially when it compares to the other algorithms. This is because the KNN algorithm will look through all of the data points before it sends out a good prediction for you to look through.

CHAPTER 20:

Support Vector Machines Classification

The SVM will be used for many challenges in regression and classification that you come across. With this one, much of the work that you do on problems with classification can make the work tricky, but this kind of algorithm can handle it all no matter what.

When working with SVM, you will be able to take each of the items that are in your data set and then plot them as one point on your n-dimensional space. N will be the number of features that we are using. Then the value of all features will translate to the value found on the coordinates. Your job here is to determine the hyperplane since this is the part that can tell you the difference between the two classes.

There will also be a few support vectors with the SVM algorithm as well, but you will also notice that these will simply end up being the coordinates of the individual observations that you have. Then you can use SVM to be the frontier that helps to separate out all the classes, and there will end up with two of them when you are done that are the line and the hyperplane.

At this point, you may be wondering what it all means and why you would want to work with an SVM. The first thing to look at is the hyperplane. There are often going to be several hyperplanes that you will need to pick from, and of course, you want to make sure that you are getting the one that works the best for your needs. This is the big challenge that comes up, but luckily the process you use will be easy. The steps that are best for helping you to work with the right hyperplane includes:

You will find that the example above is not the only time that you will be able to work with SVM to help with this type of Machine Learning. When you are taking a look at the data points that you have, and you see that there is a clear margin of separation, then the SVM method is most likely the best one to use to help you out. In addition, the effectiveness that you get out of this model will increase any time that you have a project with dimensional spaces that are pretty high. Working on this particular technique can help you to use a subset of training points that come with a decision function, or the support vector, and when the memory of the program you are working on is high enough to allow you to do this.

While there are benefits that you will get with this method depending on the project that you are working on, there are still going to be times when the SVM method is not the best for you. When you work with a data set that is large, the SVM may not provide you with options that are the most accurate. The training time with these larger sets of data can be high, and this will disappoint you if you need to get through the information quickly. And if there are some target classes that are overlapping, the SVM will behave in a way that is different than what you want.

ERIC CHAMBERLIN

CHAPTER 21:

Reinforcement Machine Learning Algorithms

Clustering, a process used to find the structure of a collection of unlabeled data, is the most important kind of unsupervised learning algorithm.

How Clustering Algorithms Work

Suppose you run a rental store and your aim is to know the preferences of your customers in order to boost your business. It is impossible for you to analyze the preferences of each individual customer and then come up with a strategy for everyone.

The best way to approach this problem is to divide your customers into a number of groups, say 8, according to their purchasing habits. A strategy should then be devised for the customers of each group. This is how clustering algorithms work.

Clustering can either be hard or soft.

In hard clustering, every data point must belong to a particular group, completely or not.

In our above example, each customer must belong to any of the 8 groups.

In soft clustering, each data point is not put into a separate cluster, but the likelihood or probability of assigning that data point to the cluster is assigned.

In our above example, every customer is assigned a probability of belonging to either of the 8 groups.

Types of Clustering Algorithms

Clustering is a subjective task, meaning that there may be many paths to the desired goal. In every methodology, a set of rules is followed for the purpose of defining the similarity between the data points.

Let's discuss some of the common clustering algorithms:

K Means Clustering

This is a clustering algorithm which works iteratively with an aim of finding the local maxima during each iteration. The algorithm follows the following steps:

i. Specify the number of clusters you wish to have, K.

ii. Assign every data point to a cluster randomly.

iii. Determine the cluster centroids.

iv. Re-assign every point to closest cluster centroid.

v. Re-computer the cluster centroids.

Repeat steps iv. and v. until there are no possible improvements. At this point global optima shall have been reached.

This will be the end of the algorithm (if the algorithm was not explicitly limited).

The following are the advantages of the K-Means clustering algorithm:

The K-Means clustering algorithm offers a fast computation if the variables are huge and K is kept small.

The algorithms can produce tighter clusters, making it easy for one to determine the relationship between the cluster members.

Disadvantages of K-Means clustering algorithm:

Predicting the value of K may be difficult.

Different initial partitions may give final clusters which are different.
It doesn't work well in cases where the clusters are of different densities and sizes.

Hierarchical Clustering

Hierarchical clustering works by creating a hierarchy of clusters. The algorithm begins with data points each of which has been assigned to its own cluster.

The two nearest clusters are then merged into a single cluster. The algorithm will terminate once only a single cluster is left.

A dendrogram is the best way to demonstrate how this clustering algorithm works. In a dendrogram, you begin with a set of data points, with each assigned to a separate cluster.

Two closest clusters are merged, and this continues until we remain with one cluster at the top of the dendrogram. The height in a dendrogram at which any two clusters are merged demonstrates the distance between the two clusters in a data space.

Advantages of Hierarchical Clustering Algorithms:

The algorithms are easy to implement and sometimes give the best results.

There is no a prior information regarding the number of clusters to be formed.

Disadvantages of Hierarchical Clustering Algorithms:

It impossible for algorithms to undo what has been done previously.

A time complexity of about $O(n2 \log n)$ is needed, with n being the number of data points.

There is no direct minimization of objective functions.

Identifying the number of clusters in the dendrogram may be difficult.

Note that K-Means is suitable when you have big data. This is because the K-Means algorithm has a linear time complexity, but a hierarchical clustering algorithm has a quadratic time complexity.

In K-Means, the number of clusters is chosen randomly, meaning that obtained results may differ from one selection of K to the next. In hierarchical clustering, we may reproduce the results.

Application of Clustering Algorithms:

- Market segmentation
- Medical imaging
- Search result grouping
- Image segmentation

- Recommendation engines
- Anomaly detection
- Social network analysis

When to use Clustering Algorithms?

Clustering algorithms should be used when one has a set of items and there is need to create some number of groups from these items.

Items which are similar are placed in the same group, while items which are different appear in separate groups.

Division of a population into either male or female is a good example of a clustering application. You may use characteristics such as hair length. Those with shorter hair might be grouped separately from these with longer hair.

Another application might be the grouping of news articles by category: business articles, politics, human interest, **etc.** Or suppose you have a number of documents written in various languages. You might use a clustering algorithm to create clusters from these documents, based upon the language used.

CHAPTER 22:

Naive Bayes -Theory

Naïve Bayes Estimation and Bayesian Networks

In the field of statistics, the probability is approached in two ways – the classical approach or the Bayesian approach. Probability is often taught using the classical approach or the frequentist approach. This is a method that is followed in all beginners' classes in statistics. In the frequentist approach to probability, mixed constants whose values are unknown are used to estimate the population parameters. These prospects are called the relative frequencies of categorical variables, and the experiment is repeated indefinitely. For example, if we toss a coin 20 times, it is not unusual to observe at least 80% heads. However, if we toss the coin 20 trillion times, we can be certain that the proportion of heads will not be that much greater than the proportion of tails. It is this behavior that defines the prospect of the frequentist approach.

However, certain situations do arise in which the classical definition of probability makes it difficult to understand the situation. For instance, what is the probability that a terrorist will strike Switzerland with a dirty bomb? Given that such an occurrence has never occurred, it is difficult to conceive what the long-term behavior of this gruesome experiment might be. Another approach to probability, the frequentist approach, uses parameters that are fixed so that the randomness lies only in the data. This randomness is viewed as a random sample from a given distribution with the unknown, but fixed, parameters.

These assumptions are turned around in the Bayesian approach to probability. In this approach to probability, the parameters are all considered to be random variables with data that is known. An assumption is made that the parameters come from a distribution of possible values, and the Bayesian approach is applied to derive some information about the parameter values.

Experts have criticized the Bayesian framework because of two potential drawbacks. First, it depends on the statistician if he or she wants to obtain the prior distribution of the dataset since different experts may provide different prior distributions. Each of these distributions will provide two different posterior distributions as results. The solution to this problem is:

If it is hard to choose the prior distribution, always choose a non-informative prior

Apply a large volume of data to diminish the need to use a prior distribution.

If neither solution works, the two posterior distributions can be tested for model efficiency and adequacy. The model with better results can be chosen.

The second criticism is the issue of scaling since Bayesian computation cannot be used to extract information on new problems since history is used as a base to derive the solution for a given problem. Bayesian analysis is hit hard by the curse of dimensionality since the normalizing factor must be integrated or summed over every possible value of the vector. This method is often infeasible if it is applied directly. The introduction of the Markov chain Monte Carlo (MCMC) methods, like the Metropolis algorithm and Gibbs sampling, have expanded the range of dimensions and problems that a machine can address using Bayesian analysis.

To help us learn how this one will work, it is time to bring out a bit of imagination. To help us with this, we are going to pretend that we are in a project that has some challenges of classification. But at the same time, you want to make sure that you can come up with a new hypothesis that will work. You will also need to figure out a design that will allow you to add in new discussions and features based on how important each variable is in this model.

This may seem like it is a lot of work to do, and like we are trying to do a lot with just one type of algorithm, it is something that we can do with this option. Once you spend a bit of time collecting the information, you will probably end up with at least a few of the shareholders and other vital investors who would like to see a model of what you plan to do and produce. And often they don't want to wait until you are all done with the work to see all of this.

As a programmer, you are going to run into a dilemma here. First, the information is not all done. And even with the information that is done, you may think that the information is too complex for someone who doesn't work in data analysis to understand, especially when it is in the beginning stage. How are you supposed to make things work for your shareholders so that they know what is going on—but make a model that isn't complete—and is easy enough to help them understand what is going on? This can be hard to do.

Often when it comes to data analysis, you are going to have thousands of points, and sometimes hundreds of thousands of points, that you are going to need to show up on your model. There could even be some new variables that show up as you are working through the training and the testing. With all of this information going on—and being in the testing stage—how are you able to take this information and present it to the shareholders quickly and in a way that is easy for them to understand what is going on?

The good thing to remember here is that there is a nice algorithm, the Naïve Bayes, that will work and help you during this early stage of the model. It is designed to present all of the information that you need, while still keeping things simple enough for anyone, even someone who isn't a data scientist, to understand. The Naïve Bayes model is meant to be easy for you to put together, and it is sometimes used to help you get through extensive sets of data in a way that is simplified. One of the advantages of working with this model is that though it is simple, it is sometimes better to work with compared to the other, more sophisticated models that you can work with. As you learn more about how to work with this algorithm, you will start to find that there are more and more reasons for you to work with it. This model is really easy to use, especially if you are a beginner to the world of deep learning and Machine Learning. You will also find that it can be effective when it is time to make some predictions for our data sets and what class they should end up in. This makes it easier for you to keep things as simple as possible during the whole process. Even though the Naïve Bayes algorithm is really simple to work with, you will find that it can perform well. When compared to some of the higher-class algorithms that are out there, and some of the ones that seem to be more sophisticated, this one is going to perform the best. However, even though there are a lot of benefits that come with the Naïve Bayes method, you need to be careful because there are a few negatives that come with it. The first negative is that when you work with an algorithm that is set with categorical variables, you need to make sure that the data you are testing hasn't already gone through a data set for training. You may find that this algorithm is going to run into some issues when it comes to making accurate predictions, and often the data sets that it assigns information to will be based more on probability than anything else. There are several different options that you can work with that are going to make this process a bit easier and will help to solve the issues that show up here, it is sometimes a bit confusing for a beginner who hasn't been able to explore and work with Machine Learning. Of course, there are a lot of things to enjoy about the Naïve Bayes algorithm, but there are some drawbacks that you need to be aware of. Remember, the Naïve Bayes is going to be able to help you do a lot of things when it comes to your presentation, but it is pretty simple. It is used as a way to show the shareholders the information that you want to present to them, but it isn't going to be able to compare the information, and it isn't able to provide the predictions that you would like—or be able to get—with some of the other options.

CHAPTER 23:

Decision Trees -Theory

Classification Using Decision Tree

Have you ever accessed to the "Ask Akinator" online game? For those who do not have a close understanding of the datasets and the data science concept, this game will appear like a kind of magic or paranormal power! In this game, you have to think about a specific character.

Then, the Blue Genni will start to ask you a series of questions like: "Is your character a YouTuber"? "Does your character really exist?" and so on. What the game do is a successful splitting of the set of characters it can deduce.

If you repeat the game for different characters you will notice that things are working in a branching principal. i.e., every answer leads to a specific set of questions that shrink the circle around the possible answer and cancel a new portion of possibilities. For example, if you answer the first question with "Yes", the game will exclude the Non-YouTuber persons from its potential decision.

The decision tree technique works just like the Akinator game; you give it a set of data and it generates answers to the game.

The decision tree is a famous and a widely used classification technique.

The decision tree concept is simple and the "How it works" can be illustrated even to people with almost no knowledge about the Machine Learning.

You may have already seen a decision tree application without knowing it is a decision tree based. In figure 3.2 a flow chart example of the decision tree.

You can notice that the flow goes in a branching manner, where finally you reach to a decision.

In this particular example, the algorithm checks for the domain of the sent email and classifies it depending on its domain.

This example is a hypothetical system. So that, if the domain is equal to MyOffice.com, the algorithm will classify it as "Urgent".

If it is not, it makes another check to ensure if the email includes the word "University".

If the text contains the word "University", then this email is categorized as "Important".

If not, the algorithm checks for the word: "Advertisement". If the email contains it, the email will be classified as "Spam". Else, it will end to the category: "To be Read later".

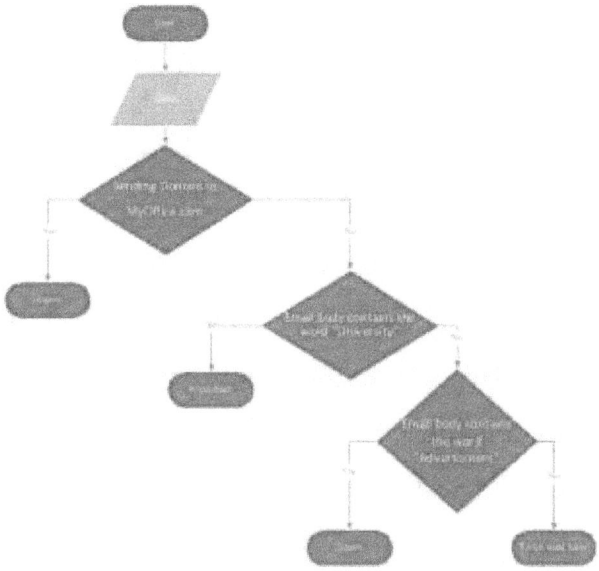

Decision tree flow chart

Note: In this figure, the diamonds are decisions that are upon some conditions. The ovals are terminations.

In this section, our decision tree algorithm will have the ability to deal with the input datasets and draw, implicitly, a tree like shown in figure 3.2. The decision tree makes a good job of translating general data into a useful knowledge. The decision tree Machine Learning algorithm creates rules that classify the unfamiliar datasets. Decision trees are common in expert systems, and they give perfect results compared to those produced by human expert with long periods of experience in a certain field.

Decision Tree Construction

Before applying the decision tree algorithm to a dataset, we first need to specify the feature the splitting process will be based on. If you do not have a clear idea about the most feature that rule the dataset, you may try different suggested features until you get the best results. This results in subsets out of the original dataset. Practically, each subset represents a desired feature. Therefore, the subsets keep splitting depending on the features as they travel down the branches. When the data on the branches is the same class, we have classified it and we do not have to continue the splitting process. Else, the algorithm has to be repeated until we have classified all the data. The decision tree algorithm is summarized in table 3.3. From the table, you can notice the recursive nature of the algorithm; as it calls itself until all data is classified. A python code will be written throughout our talk about the decision tree section.

A common way of splitting data in the decision tree is the binary split. But suppose that we have followed the binary way, but we still have other possible features, for much more splits. Therefore, in this section we will utilize the ID3 algorithm [9]. This algorithm helps in making rules about how to split the data and when to stop.

Decision Tree Algorithm

- Each object in the given dataset is in the same class/category.

- If Yes, return the name/label of the category

- Else, try another feature to divide the dataset

- Make a new a branch node

- For every divide iteration

Call the "decision tree algorithm" and add the results to the new branch node

Return branch node

The decision tree algorithm works with both numeric and nominal values. It is simple in terms of computational complexity and of understanding the learnt results. Moreover, it is robust against missing values and can handle features that are irrelevant.

However, the main disadvantage of the decision tree algorithm is that it is prone to overfitting. Overfitting is a common defect in the decision tree and other classification algorithms.

It occurs when make multiple hypothesis about the training data, **i.e.** assigning meaningful values to noise. This indeed reduces the errors in the training dataset but at the expense of the testing dataset. In other words, an overfit model is too specific to its training data. So that, when it deals with a new data, its prediction error in this new data is at risk of being very high.

CHAPTER 24:

Benefits of Machine Learning

When businesses perform analyses, they use large volumes of data, and they prefer using real-time data to perform those analyses. It is difficult for human beings to analyze that volume of data. Therefore, Machine Learning makes it easier to analyze with ease.

Machine learning is improving day by day. Now that most engineers are integrating Machine Learning with deep learning, they are reducing the cost of data engineering and data preprocessing.

Data mining and Machine Learning are closely knit. The former refers to the process of sifting through large volumes of data to identify the necessary relationships and correlations that exist within the data set.

It helps the machine identify the necessary information from a large data set. There are many occasions where it is impossible for a human being to design a machine with a set of specific conditions within which a machine can function well.

For most machines, the external conditions tend to have an adverse effect on the performance. In these situations, it is good to use Machine Learning to acclimatize the machine to the environment since this ensures that the system maintains its efficiency. Machine learning will also help the machine adapt to changes in the environment.

Many problems can arise if a programmer has to hardcode an elaborate process into the system; it is possible that the programmer may miss a few details. When there is a manual error in the code, it becomes very difficult for the programmer to encode the program all over again into the system. In these instances, it is best to allow the machine to learn the process.

The technology industry is constantly changing, and every new change gives rise to a new language that can be used as well. It does not make sense to redesign a system simply because a new change has been made in the industry, especially when many changes are being made. It is in these instances that Machine Learning helps the system acclimatize to these changes.

CHAPTER 25:

Deep Neutral Network

Neural networks

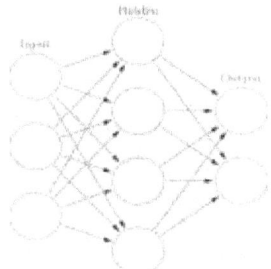

You can also work with neural networks when it comes to unsupervised Machine Learning. These types of networks will be used a lot because they are great at learning and analyzing patterns by looking at it in several different layers. Each layer that it goes through will spend its time seeing if there is a pattern that is inside the image. If the neural network does find a new pattern, it will activate the process to help the next layer start. This process will continue going on and on until all the layers in that algorithm are created, and the program can predict what is in the image.

Now, there will be several things that will happen from this point. If the algorithm went through all the layers and then was able to use that information to make an accurate prediction, the neurons will become stronger. This results in a good association between the patterns and the object and the system will be more efficient at doing this the next time you use the program.

This may seem a bit complicated so let's take a look at how these neural networks will work together. Let's say that you are trying to create a program that can take the input of a picture and then recognize that there is a car in that picture. It will be able to do this based on the features that are in the car, including the color of the car, the number on the license plate, and even more.

When you are working with some of the conventional coding methods that are available, this process can be really difficult to do. You will find that the neural network system can make this a really easy system to work with.

For the algorithm to work, you would need to provide the system with an image of the car. The neural network would then be able to look over the picture. It would start with the first layer, which would be the outside edges of the car. Then it would go through a number of other layers that help the neural network understand if there were any unique characteristics that are present in the picture that outlines that it is a car. If the program is good at doing the job, it will get better at finding some of the smallest details of the car, including things like its windows and even wheel patterns.

There could potentially be a lot of different layers that come with this one, but the more layers and details that the neural network can find, the more accurately it will be able to predict what kind of car is in front of it. If your neural network is accurate in identifying the car model, it will learn from this lesson. It will remember some of these patterns and characteristics that showed up in the car model and will store them for use later. The next time that they encounter the same kind of car model, they will be able to make a prediction pretty quickly.

This particular algorithm is one that will often be used when you are trying to go through pictures and sort out defining features. It could be used as a face recognition software where you wouldn't be able to put in all of the information ahead of time. It works for defining car models, recognizing different animals, and more.

One of the advantages that you will enjoy when you use neural networks is that you won't have to worry about all of the statistical training for this kind of algorithm. Even without the statistics, you will be able to use it to find some of the complex relationships that show up between the dependent and the independent variables, even if these are nonlinear. The biggest issue with using the neural networks is that they will have a pretty high computational cost so it is not always feasible to use them as much as you would like.

There are a few things that could happen when you enter this point, based on how the program is working. If the algorithm was able to go through the process above, and it did a good job at sorting through the layers, it will then provide you with a prediction. If the program is right in its prediction, the neurons of this system just like the neurons in the brain are going to become stronger.

The reason that this works so well is that the program decided to work with Artificial Intelligence, which allowed it to make strong associations between the object and the patterns that it found. The more times that the system can look at a picture and come back with the right answer, the more efficient it is going to be the next time you use it.

Any time that a programmer wants to work with the neural network algorithm, you will often be working with things like face recognition software and other similar projects. When this happens, all of the information that you and the program need won't be available ahead of time. But you can use this method to teach the system the best way to recognize the right faces in the image. You can also use this one to help with different types of animals, to define models of cars, and so much more.

As you can imagine reading through this chapter, there are a lot of different advantages that come with this particular model when working on Machine Learning. One of the advantages that you are going to notice is that you can utilize these methods without having to control the statistics of the algorithm. Even if you need to use it without the statistics being available, the neural network will still be able to finish the work for you. The reason that this ends up working so well is that both the dependent and the independent variable are going to be nonlinear.

There are a few times when you will not want to work with this method. One of the main reasons that programmers would choose not to go with a neural network is that it is also one of those models that has a high computing cost to get the information. For some of the smaller businesses who are interested in working with Machine Learning and doing this kind of technology, the cost is going to take too much time, computational power, and money and they will need to look at some other algorithms instead.

Feedforward Neural Networks

The first and most simple form of Neural Networks is called feedforward. As the name implies, data flows through a feedforward network in one direction, from the input, through the node layers containing the neurons and exits through the output layer. Unlike more modern neural networks, feedforward networks do not cycle or iterate over their data. They perform a single operation on the input data, and they provide their solution in an output stream.

Single-layer perceptron

This is the simplest form of a feedforward neural network with one layer of nodes. The input is sent to each node already weighted and depending on how the node calculates the input and its weight, a minimal threshold may or not be met, and the neuron either fires (taking the "activated" value) or does not fire (taking the "deactivated" value).

Multi-layer Perceptron

Multi-layer Perceptrons, as the name suggests, are consist of two or more (sometimes many more) layers, with the output of the upper layer becoming the input of the lower layer. Because there are many layers, this form of neural network often takes advantage of backpropagation, where the produced output is compared with the expected output, and the degree of error fed backward through the network to adjust the weights on the appropriate nodes, all with the intention of producing an output closer to the desired output state. Each error correction is tiny, so often a great number of iterations are required to achieve a "learned" state. At this point, the neural network is no longer considered a feedforward system proper. It is algorithms such as these multi-layer networks with backpropagation that have become some of the most successful and powerful Machine Learning devices in the field.

Recurrent Neural Networks

Recurrent Neural Networks propagate data in both directions, forward like feedforward networks but also backward from later to earlier processing stages. One of the main strengths of recurrent neural networks is the ability to remember previous states. Before recurrent neural networks, a neural network would forget previous tasks once it was asked to begin a new one. Imagine reading a comic but forgetting the content of the previous cells as you read the next one. Recurrent neural networks allow information to persist, meaning they can take input from subsequent events and "remember" their experience in previous ones. Put simply, recurrent neural networks are a series of input and output networks with the output of the first becoming the input of the second, the second's output the input of the third, and so on. This cycling allows Recurrent Neural Networks to develop closer and closer approximations to the desired output.

Backpropagation

Theoretical development of backpropagation came from Paul Werbos' Ph.D. thesis in 1974. Unfortunately, due to complications and difficulties encountered by those attempts to create Neural Networks (both theoretical and hardware-related), Neural Networks did not really catch on until the 1980s, when processor power and large numerous data sets became available for training and testing.

The application of backpropagation is highly mathematical but can be summarized like this: each iteration of a neural network produces a mathematical degree of error between the desired output and the actual output of the network. Each neuron in a neural network has a weight attached to it for the purposes of modifying its calculation on the input it receives. Backpropagation uses mathematics (probability statistics) when it is possible, to calculate the derivative of the error between expected and actual outputs. This derivative is then used on the next iteration to adjust the weight applied to each of the neurons. Each subsequent iteration produces a smaller error. Imagine a basketball dropped somewhere in a skateboard half-pipe. It will roll down towards the center and up the other side, then reverse direction and roll towards the center again. Each time, it will roll less distance up the side before reversing direction. Eventually, gravity will bring the ball to a stable state in the center. In the same way, backpropagation reduces the error produced in each iteration as it brings the actual output closer to the desired output.

We have seen above that the goal of Machine Learning is to make software able to learn from the data it experiences. This is the goal of Neural Networks as well, but while Machine Learning makes decisions based on what data it has seen before, Neural Networks are designed to learn and make intelligent decisions on their own. This is particularly useful when the patterns being searched for are too numerous or complex for a software programmer to extract and submit as part of an input training data set.

CHAPTER 26:

Big Data Analytics

Big Data is pretty much what it sounds like — the practice of dealing with large volumes of data. And by large, we are talking about astoundingly huge amounts of data — gigabytes, terabytes, petabytes of data. A petabyte, to put this size into perspective, is 10 to the 15th bytes. Written out that is 1 PB = 1,000,000,000,000,000 bytes. When you consider that a single byte is equivalent in storage to a single letter like an 'a' or 'x', the scale of the data sets being dealt with my Big Data is truly awe-inspiring. And these sizes are increasing every day.

The term Big Data comes from the 1990s, although computer scientists have been dealing with large volumes of data for decades. What sets Big Data apart from data sets before is the fact the size of data sets began to overwhelm the ability of traditional data analytics software to deal with it. New database storage systems had to be created (Hadoop for example) just to hold the data and new software written to be able to deal with so much information in a meaningful way.

Today the term Big Data brings with it a series of assumptions and practices that have made it a field all its own. Most Big Data discussions begin with the 3 V's. Big data is data containing more variety arriving in increasing volumes and with increasing velocity (acceleration would be an accurate term to use here, but then we'd lose the alliteration).

Volume

The term volume refers to the vast amount of data available. When the term Big Data was coined in the early 2000s, the amount of data available for analysis was overwhelming. Since then, the volume of data created has grown exponentially. In fact, the volume of data produced has become so vast then new storage solutions had to be created just to deal with it. This increase in available data shows no sign of slowing and is, in fact, increasing geometrically by doubling every two years.

Velocity

Along with the rise in the amount of data being created is the speed at which it is produced. Things like smartphones, RFID chips, and real-time facial recognition produce not only enormous amounts of data, this data is produced in real time and must be dealt with as it is created. If not processed in real time, it must be stored for later processing. The increasing speed of this data arriving strains the capacity of bandwidth, processing power, and storage space to contain it for later use.

Variety

Data does not get produced in a single format. It is stored numerically in detailed databases, produced in structure-less text and email documents, and stored digitally in streaming audio and video. There is stock market data, financial transactions, and so on, all of it uniquely structured. So not only must large amounts of data be handled very quickly, it is produced in many formats that require distinct methods of handling for each type.

Lately, two more V's have been added:

Value

Data is intrinsically valuable, but only if you are able to extract this value from it. Also, the state of input data, whether it is nicely structured in a numeric database or unstructured text message chains, affects its value. The less structure a data set has, the more work needs to be put into it before it can be processed. In this sense, well-structured data is more valuable than less-structured data.

Veracity

Not all captured data is of equal quality. When dealing with assumptions and predictions parsed out of large data sets, knowing the veracity of the data being used has an important effect on the weight given to the information studying it generates. There are many causes that limit data veracity. Data can be biased by the assumptions made by those who collected it. Software bugs can introduce errors and omission in a data set. Abnormalities can reduce data veracity like when two wind speed sensors next to each other report different wind directions. One of the sensors could be failing, but there is no way to determine this from data itself. Sources can also be of questionable veracity — in a company's social media feed are a series of very negative reviews. Were they human or bot created? Human error, as in a person signing up to a web service enters their phone number incorrectly. And there are many more ways data veracity can be compromised.

The point of dealing with all this data is to identify useful detail out of all the noise — businesses can find ways to reduce costs, increase speed and efficiency, design new products and brands, and make more intelligent decisions. Governments can find similar benefits in studying the data produced by their citizens and industries.

Current uses of Big Data.

Product Development

Big Data can be used to predict customer demand. Using current and past products and services to classify key attributes, they can then model these attributes' relationships and their success in the market.

Predictive Maintenance

Buried in structured data are indices that can predict mechanical failure of machine parts and systems. Year of manufacture make and model, and so on, provide a way to predict future breakdowns. Also, there is a wealth of unstructured data in error messages, service logs, operating temperature, and sensor data. This data, when correctly analyzed, can predict problems before they happen so maintenance can be deployed preemptively, reducing both cost and system downtime.

Customer Experience

Many businesses are nothing without their customers. Yet acquiring and keeping customers in a competitive landscape is challenging and expensive. Anything that can give a business an edge will be eagerly utilized. Using Big Data, businesses can get a much clearer view of the customer experience by examining social media, website visit metrics, call logs, and any other recorded customer interaction to modify and improve the customer experience. All in the interests of maximizing the value delivered in order to acquire and maintain customers. Offers to individual customers can become not only more personalized but more relevant and accurate. By using Big Data to identify problematic issues, businesses can handle them quickly and effectively, reducing customer churn and negative press.

Fraud & Compliance

While there may be single rogue bad actors out there in the digital universe attempting to crack system security, the real threats are from organized, well-financed teams of experts, sometimes teams supported by foreign governments. At the same time, security practices and standards never stand still but are constantly changing with new technologies and new approaches to hacking existing ones. Big Data helps identify data patterns suggesting fraud or tampering and aggregation of these large data sets makes regulatory reporting much faster.

Operation Efficiency

Not the sexiest topic, but this is the area in which Big Data is currently providing the most value and return. Analyze and assess production systems, examine customer feedback and product returns, and examine a myriad of other business factors to reduce outages and waste, and even anticipate future demand and trends. Big Data is even useful in assessing current decision-making processes and how well they function in meeting demand.

Innovation

Big Data is all about relations between meaningful labels. For a large business, this can mean examining how people, institutions, other entities, and business processes intersect, and use any interdependencies to drive new ways to take advantage of these insights. New trends can be predicted, and existing trends can be better understood. This all leads to understanding what customers actually want and anticipate what they may want in the future. Knowing enough about individual customers may lead to the ability to take advantage of dynamic pricing models. Innovation driven by Big Data is really only limited by the ingenuity and creativity of the people curating it.

Machine Learning is also meant to deal with large amounts of data very quickly. But while Big Data is focused on using existing data to find trends, outliers, and anomalies, Machine Learning uses this same data to "learn" these patterns in order to deal with future data proactively. While Big Data looks to the past and present data, Machine Learning examines the present data to learn how to deal with the data that will be collected in the future. In Big Data, it is people who define what to look for and how to organize and structure this information. In Machine Learning, the algorithm teaches itself what is important through iteration over test data, and when this process is completed, the algorithm can then go ahead to new data it has never experienced before.

ERIC CHAMBERLIN

CHAPTER 27:

Data Mining and Applications

What's the point of ads? They're on our monitors, TV screens and smartphone displays, inside our favorite radio broadcasts and mailboxes. No matter where we turn, we'll find ads constantly hawking something we're not interested in. Those ads represent the traditional shotgun approach where companies simply propel as many as they can in our general direction and hope at least one hits. As we can imagine, this kind of marketing costs a lot, but companies just don't know any better and keep pumping money into wacky, bizarre and embarrassing ads, hoping anything works. Thanks to Machine Learning we might be nearing a future where computers produce dirt cheap ads that are scarily tailored to our behavior and applied at the exact moment when they'll have the strongest effect. In fact, we might already be living in one such future.

One thing about consumer behavior is that most purchases are done automatically, but there are major life events that can break these habits and put us on the cusp of trying new things. This means Fig Newtons ads aren't necessarily aimed at people who'd never try Fig Newtons but at those who like sweets and might try something different because they're undergoing a major life event, such as divorce, car purchase or pregnancy. How does the advertising company know which person is which? Enter data mining, harvesting as much data about people to have computers try and predict their behavior, desires and motivations to target them with just the right kind of ad at just the right moment. Of course, ads would never work on us, but machines can learn to be persuasive.

One thing to note here is that the processes of data mining are going to be used to help us build up Machine Learning models. These models that rely on Machine Learning are able to power up applications, including the recommendation programs found on many websites, and the technology that is able to keep search engines running.

How Does Data Mining Work?

So, why is data mining such an important process to focus on? You will see the staggering numbers when it comes to the volume of data that is produced is doubling every two years. Just by looking at unstructured data on its own, but just because we have more of this information doesn't mean that we have more knowledge all of the time. With the help of data mining, you are able to do some of the following tasks:

- Sift through all of the noise, whether it is repetitive or chaotic, that is found in your data.

- You are able to understand better what is relevant in all of that information, and then make good use of the information to help you assess what outcomes are the most likely for your needs.

- It can help you to accelerate the pace of making decisions that are informed and driven by data, and more likely to help your business to thrive and grow.

Now that we have that figured out, it is time to take a look at how all of this data mining is going to work. We are not going to just grab the data, and then these trends will show up with us having to do no more work on them. And this is where we will be able to work with data mining. Data mining is a great way for us to explore and then analyze a large amount of information with the goal of finding all of the insights, trends, and patterns that we are able to use out of that information.

For example, we are able to work with data mining to help us to learn more about the opinions and even the sentiment of the users, to help us learn how to properly detect fraud, to help out with risk management, filtering the spam out of email, and even with marketing. All of these are going to be important to many different kinds of companies, and when you use them properly, you will find that they are going to ensure that you can better serve your customers over time.

There are five basic steps that we are going to see when it comes to working with data mining. In the first step, the company is going to spend some time collecting the data they want to use, and then they will make sure that all of this is going to be loaded up in the proper manner to their data warehouse. When this is all done, the company can then store and manage the data. Sometimes this is done on the in-house servers of the company, and other times it is going to be sent to the cloud.

When we go through with this, the management teams, IT professionals, and even business analysts are going to be able to gain access to this data, and then they can determine the way that they would like to organize all of this information. We are then able to work with application software in order to sort out the data based on the results that the user is going to put in. In the last step, our end-user is going to be able to present their findings and all of that information in a certain format that makes the most sense, and that will be easy for those in charge of making decisions to read through and understand.

While we are on this topic, we need to work on something that is known as data warehousing and mining software. The different programs that you decide to use with data mining are going to be responsible for analyzing the patterns, as well as the relationships, that we are able to find in the data, and all of this is going to be done based on the requests that the user sends out. It is possible that a company is going to use this software to help them create some new classes on that information.

We are able to go through and illustrate this point a bit more, as well. Let's imagine that we are a restaurant that would like to work with all of the steps of data mining in order to determine the right times to offer some specials. The restaurant would be able to do this by looking at all of the information they have been able to collect that is on the specials, and then see how the specials do at different times of the days and on different days of the week. They can then go through and create classes based on when the customers visit, and what the customer is most likely to order when they do come to the restaurant to eat.

We are able to take this to the next level as well. In some cases, a data miner is going to be able to find clusters of information based on a logical relationship, or they may take some time to see if there are sequential patterns and associations that they are able to draw some conclusions to learn more about their customers in the long run.

Warehousing is going to be another important part that we see with the data mining process. This is a pretty simple process to work with, and it is basically going to include when a company is able to centralize their data into one database or one program, rather than spreading out the information in more than one place. With the warehouse for data, an organization is able to spinoff some of the segments of the data for the right users to look over and analyze on a regular basis, and for the specific users to gain access to when they need it.

However, there are also times when we will see that the analyst will take the work on a different course during this process. For example, the analyst may choose to start out with some of the data they find the most useful, and then they will be able to create their own warehouse for the data based on the specifications there. No matter how a business wants to organize their data, they are going; they can definitely use it to help support some of the decision processes that the management of that company is going to make.

With this in mind, we also need to take some time to explore examples of data mining along the way. A good example of this is grocery stores. Many of the supermarkets that we visit on a regular basis give away free loyalty cards to customers. These are beneficial to the customers because it provides them with access to prices that are reduced, and other special deals that non-members at that store are not going to be able to get.

But these cards are also going to be beneficial for the store as well because it is going to make it easier for the company to track which customers are buying what, when they are in the store making the purchase, and at what price they are making the purchases for. After receiving all of this data and having a chance to analyze it the stores can then use this kind of data to offer customers coupons targeted to those buying habits, and they decide when to put certain items on sale, or when it is best for the company to sell them at full price.

This is a great way for both parties to win. The customer is going to enjoy that they can potentially save money and so they will sign up for it. The store is going to enjoy that they get a chance to learn more about the customers and set prices at a point that will bring in more people and make them the most money possible.

Here, we need to keep in mind that there are at times a few concerns that data mining is able to bring up for the customer and for a company. Some customers are concerned about this process of data mining because they worry about the company not being ethical with their use of the data at all. It could even be an issue with a legitimate and honest company because the sampling they use could be wrong, and then they are going to use the wrong kind of information to make their decisions.

Most companies need to take some caution when they decide to work with the data mining process to ensure that they are going to be able to reach their customers better and do well in their industry through some useful insights and more that they are able to learn along the way. It is definitely something that you need to focus on when it is time to learn what patterns and insights are found in all of that data.

All of this data is going to be important when it comes to working in the process of data science. But we have to make sure that we really understand how this data is supposed to work and what is actually found inside of all that data. When we are able to learn all of this, we will find that it is easier than we may think in order to handle the data and get it to work for our needs.

Unbalanced Data Set

Although imbalanced data is a common problem with datasets, there is no universal technique for dealing with this issue. Generally, when classifiers are fed imbalanced data, the classification output will be biased, resulting in always predicting the majority class and incorrectly classifying the minority class. Therefore, we need to detect when the output is biased and deal with this issue, to improve the accuracy of the models. We will over-sample the minority class by employing the Synthetic Minority Over-sampling Technique (SMOTE) along with the stratified K-Fold cross validation method, for dealing with the class imbalance.

Conclusion

Thank you for making it through to the end of this book. The next step is to start using some of the different techniques and tools that we can work through to utilize Python Machine Learning. The field of Machine Learning is growing like crazy. Many computer programmers are interested in learning more about how this works, as well as how they can use it, to see the best results and to help them create new technology into the future. Think of it—a few years ago, there were no such things as the Alexa device (and other similar software from other companies) that could listen to your commands and respond—and that is all thanks to Machine Learning!

This guidebook took some time to look at both the Python language and Machine Learning, as well as some of the different algorithms that you will be able to use with both of these. By the time you get to this point, you should be well-versed in some of the different algorithms that you can work with, as well as how they are going to benefit you based on the Machine Learning project you would like to work with!

While this step-by-step guide demonstrates the most popular Machine Learning algorithms and techniques, you also need to hone your research skills. This is a wide field, and there is no single source that provides you with everything you need. In addition, Machine Learning is constantly evolving, which means you need to know how to keep up with it. This may sound discouraging at first, but you should look at it as a challenge that will help you grow as a person and as an entry-level machine learner.

With the help of this book, you already took the most important step by learning how to find and import datasets, and you also developed a toolkit that holds enough powerful and versatile tools to help you solve many of the most common Machine Learning problems. Furthermore, you explored the most important supervised and unsupervised Machine Learning algorithms, such as regression, k-means clustering, k-nearest neighbors, and the principal component analysis, together with artificial neural networks, such as the restricted Boltzmann machine. You have also gone step by step through a number of examples written in Python and learned how to put these algorithms to use. Machine learning may be challenging, but it is mostly about knowing the right tools for the job.

Keep in mind that this subject is fairly complex and even taking a small step to meet this challenge is something you should be proud of. The purpose of this book is to teach you the basics and provide you with the necessary tools to help you further pursue your Machine Learning goals. Just make sure to put everything you learn into practice; otherwise, the foundation you started building will not hold for long. This is a field that has nothing to do with talent, only persistence and motivation.

You have everything you need to pursue your interest in Machine Learning, so continue onwards and practice, practice, practice!

With some knowledge of basic Python, Machine Learning skills, and Python libraries, you are now set to launch your first Machine Learning project with Python. Consider learning the open-source Python libraries. The scientific Python libraries will help you complete easy Machine Learning tasks. However, the choice of some of these libraries can be completely subjective and highly debatable by many people in the industry.

Just like how a child learns how to walk is the same with learning Machine Learning with Python. You need to practice many times before you can become better. Practice different algorithms and use different datasets to improve your knowledge and overall problem-solving skills.

The best way to go about this is to begin working on simple problem statements and solve them using the different algorithms that are mentioned in this book. You can also try to solve these problems by identifying newer ways to solve the problem. Once you get a hang of the basic problems, you can try using some advanced methods to solve those problems.

When you are ready to learn more about how the Python coding language and Machine Learning work together and when you want to learn how to make Python Machine Learning work for your needs, then make sure to check out this guidebook to help you get started!

www.ingramcontent.com/pod-product-compliance
Lightning Source LLC
Chambersburg PA
CBHW071401210526
45465CB00001B/206